Planning and Designing the Absent City

This book concerns the study of open-air accommodation facilities. The market evolutions allow us to look at these structures as temporary settlements characterised by a low-density dwelling and a close connection with natural elements and the landscape.

This new and different point of view is sustained by the tendency of outdoor tourism to go in the direction of temporary villages, and this tendency is directly related to "time" and "landscape". The landscape is the reason why the campsite is settled. The time is linked to the holiday season timing. Today, both are greatly influenced by the introduction of the "Maxi-Caravan". This removable living unit can be placed on an empty pitch, occupying the landscape without ruining the soil. By the settlement of Maxi-Caravans, the campsite is transformed from an empty landscape with tents to a temporary settlement, whose timing is divided between the seasonal timing of the campsite and the "timing" of the product, and whose landscape is organised by the relation with the prevalent landscape and the internal one. The book's core defines the outdoor facility structure, using Italy as the main case study. To identify design strategies, the book analyses temporary settlement examples (quick time) and projects from historic outdoor tourism (medium time). Finally, the last chapter reflects on open-air accommodation facilities by showing their applicability in the different contexts of refugee camps (long time).

The aim of this research is to enhance the theme of open-air accommodation facilities, highlighting the need to equalise the study of temporary settlements with that of permanent settlements. It will be of interest to researchers and students of planning, landscape and tourism.

Luca Trabattoni is Associate Professor at the Opole University of Technology (Poland), belonging to the Department of Architecture and Planning since 2018, where he teaches Landscape and Interior Design. He is an on contract professor for the courses of Architectural Composition at the Polytechnic of Milan and at the University of Pavia, Faculty of Engineering and Architecture and for the course of Materials Technology at the NABA (New Academy of Fine Arts) in Milan. He is a freelancer and co-founder of "ARCò architecture and cooperation" that studies the approach to emergency architecture in relation to the theme of sustainability, realising building all over the world. ARCò's work has been published in various international journals and has received numerous awards. He collaborates with the AUDE research laboratory of the University of Pavia, co-coordinating the research project on Mobile Homes. He founded "Camp Design and Architecture" to develop the theme of landscape design for campsites.

Planning and Designing the Absent City

Campsites as Temporary Settlements

Luca Trabattoni

LONDON AND NEW YORK

First published 2025
by Routledge
4 Park Square, Milton Park, Abingdon, Oxon OX14 4RN

and by Routledge
605 Third Avenue, New York, NY 10158

Routledge is an imprint of the Taylor & Francis Group, an informa business

British Library Cataloguing-in-Publication Data
A catalogue record for this book is available from the British Library

Library of Congress Cataloging-in-Publication Data
Names: Trabattoni, Luca, author.
Title: Planning and designing the absent city : campsites as
temporary settlements / Luca Trabattoni.
Description: Abingdon, Oxon ; New York, NY : Routledge, 2025. |
Includes bibliographical references and index.
Identifiers: LCCN 2024015648 (print) | LCCN 2024015649 (ebook) |
ISBN 9781032742847 (hardback) | ISBN 9781032742854 (paperback) |
ISBN 9781003468530 (ebook)
Subjects: LCSH: Camp sites, facilities, etc.–Design and construction. |
Temporary structures (Building) | Refugee camps. | Tourism–Social aspects.
Classification: LCC GV198.L3 T73 2025 (print) |
LCC GV198.L3 (ebook) | DDC 647.942–dc23/eng/20240410
LC record available at https://lccn.loc.gov/2024015648
LC ebook record available at https://lccn.loc.gov/2024015649

ISBN: 978-1-032-74284-7 (hbk)
ISBN: 978-1-032-74285-4 (pbk)
ISBN: 978-1-003-46853-0 (ebk)

DOI: 10.4324/9781003468530

Typeset in Times New Roman
by Newgen Publishing UK

This book is the result of research begun together with Professor Carlo Berizzi and the members of the AUDe lab of the University of Pavia and the collaboration of the friends of Crippaconcept. It would not have been possible without the serious and loving help of M.

Contents

Figures

Introduction

Since 2020, the pandemic wave that swept the world has coercively conditioned the ways of inhabiting for various populations. Compulsory quarantine, along with the reduced mobility caused by it, albeit with variations adopted in various European and non-European countries, imposed a period of life in which "dwelling" meant "inhabiting domestic space". The constrained spatial dimension, in most cases, highlighted the value of the dimensions of domestic spaces and, in particular, the vital relationship between open space and the natural context. Even in less extreme contexts, reduced possibilities for "escape" have generated an even greater need for open spaces.

In Italy, the phenomenon of "balconies" was emblematic of this, occupied even when they were very small in order to demonstrate a sense of collectivity and solidarity. Hundreds of people took to the balconies of Italy to sing and play music in a collective sign of resistance to the pandemic. The outside itself is a site of co-presence as well as breathing space, and the idea of the outside being linked to dwelling once again became a contingent theme in everyday domesticities and the extraordinary, such as vacations and travelling.

It is easy to see how that rediscovery of the outside induced by the constraints of the pandemic clashes with issues inherent in everyday domesticity. When not present in the domestic space, the "exterior" has thus been sought elsewhere, away from the everyday. Therefore, it is unsurprising that this search, or rediscovery of nature, has also resonated with how people travel to experience their vacations. The outdoor tourism market represents the expression of this need for a renewed relationship with nature and open space well. Outdoor

DOI: 10.4324/9781003468530-1

tourism in recent years has been experiencing a vital quantitative and qualitative evolution.

Since 2018, together with the *AUDe*[1] Laboratory of the University of Pavia and Professor *Carlo Berizzi*, we have been researching the directions of this evolution, specifically within the Italian territory, concerning sensitive issues such as landscape protection and Sustainability. The research "*Mobile Homes for Sustainable Tourism*[2]", promoted together with the company *Crippaconcept*[3], led to the organisation of some design workshops and scientific publications that developed the theme of the "Maxi-Caravan" (which we will revisit later) integrated into the landscape of the campsite. This has also led to the compilation of a descriptive manual on this industrial product[4] and a prototype Maxi-Caravan called *Wonderland*[5] being built, with its components made to be as sustainable as possible.The research also initiated a design experience called Camping Design and Architecture[6], which develops design plans for campsites and whose experience to date, developed from more than 50 cases, has provided a basis for reflection for this discussion.

If the tourism system is assimilable to the concept of a city (Trillo, 2003), the system of open-air accommodations represents a particular settlement system characterised by a particular temporality and a specific relationship with the landscape. In fact, it is possible to consider it, due to the number of people and the area occupied, as an intermittent city that is only occupied during the summer months and then remains dormant during the rest of the year. In fact, outdoor tourism, that of campsites and resorts, when compared to other forms of use, experiences a strong constraint due to seasonality. On average, accommodations open in April/May and close in September/October. This seasonal temporality is crucial in defining the way of using the land and natural space, two values intrinsic to this type of tourism.

Open-air facilities enhance the void, relate to the "prevailing" landscape, and provide different ways to inhabit a naturalised context. For this reason, removability characterises the elements that define this settlement system. Whether owned by the tourist himself or the facility, the housing units that make up the settlement relate to the landscape in a transitive way. This sui generis city is therefore definable as "temporary" in two different ways, as we shall see below. However, this characterising bond with nature is the reason why, less so than other forms of tourism, it has suffered damage as a result of the pandemic.

The necessary comparison becomes that of living in nature, shifting the attention from the touristic, experiential aspect of the campsite to the settlement one. The morphological approach then becomes substantial because the construction of the internal landscape, linked to the current evolution of the campsite, is determined by the relationship between built and unbuilt. The built environment is represented by Maxi-Caravans, a removable industrial product characterising the development of open-air accommodation facilities.

This housing system works like a foundation city, given that thanks to the characteristics of the industrial product (i.e. no foundation), it is installed in empty areas. The immediate appeal is that it is linked to the history of utopian cities, from Moore to Howard, and temporary settlement systems. These housing systems, which in human history often coincide with nomadic cultures, have a "contemporary version" linked to events (religious and non-religious festivals) and emergencies (refugee camps, informal cities, slums).

People

According to data published by Eurostat, in 2019, the tourist accommodation system of campsites in the EU28 area numbered 29,454 structures for a total of almost 10 million beds. However, as can be read in the FAITA[7] report on open-air tourism, produced by CISET (International Centre for Studies on the Tourism Economy),

> In 2021, as a result of the United Kingdom's exit from the European Union (which, in 2016, housed over 4,700 open-air facilities and 1.4 million beds) and the pandemic, their number is estimated to have dropped to 23,753 units for approximately 8.4 million beds. In reality, if we consider the historical series from 2012 to 2021 after the United Kingdom – therefore 27 countries –, the consistency of open-air accommodation has grown in almost ten years, going from 21,852 structures in 2012 to 23,753 in 2021 (+0. 9% annual average).

This represents around 4% of the total European accommodation offered in terms of establishments, but approximately 30% with reference to bed places.

In the world of tourism, the pandemic has had a significant impact, linked first to the limitations of transactional travel and a change in market demand trends. As can be read on the EUROSTAT website, although there is a decrease in tourist attendance, which was inevitable during the pandemic period, the open-air tourism sector has reacted less catastrophically than other sectors.

Covid consequences	*April/ September 2020*	*International tourism*	*Domestic tourism*	*Hotel*	*Campsite*
Gap of number of nights in 2019	56%	-74%	-38%	-63%	**-38%**

When looking at the number of nights spent in EU campsites by domestic tourists, the situation differs. In contrast to the general development, the number of nights spent increased in 10 EU Member States (with available data) between April and September 2020 compared with the same period in 2019. Slovenia recorded the highest increase (+76%), followed by Austria (+32%) and Belgium (+25%)[8].

Italy is among the highest European nations for arrivals and presence of tourists. It represents an emblematic case of the number of people in the territory and the economic value of the tourism sector within the national economy. According to "*the Outdoor Tourism Observatory | Summer 2023 Forecasts*", created by Human Company and Thrends, "The 2023 summer season of outdoor tourism will see 56.6 million visitors for the months of June, July, August and September, increasing by 2% compared to 2022 (55.5 million) and by 1% compared to 2019 (55.9 million)." The influx of tourists relating to outdoor tourism (campsites, villages and the like) has seen an increase compared to the post-pandemic period, but without reaching the levels of the pre-pandemic one (2019), however it does demonstrate a clear growing trend. Furthermore, according to the latest report drawn up by Human Company and Thrends (using ISTAT, EUROSTAT data and the Statistical data of the Italian Reasons), *the flows of tourist presence have further increased, demonstrating the significant role of this type of tourism in the Italian market*[9].

	2019	*2020*	*2021*	*2022*
Number of peoples (in billions)	66,8	37,5	54,6	66,1
Local	33,7	25,1	30,2	31,9
Foreign	33,1	12,4	24,4	34,3

Environment

Quantitatively, the data demonstrate the tourism sector's impact in Europe and Italy. However, the quality of the service is also evolving, linked to changes in requests from increasingly numerous audiences and to the formation of an ethical conscience concerning the protection and respect of the environment.

There has been a change in this type of holiday characterised by two aspects: on the one hand, the demand for "luxury" and high-level services has increased; on the other, sensitivity towards the issue of sustainability has also increased. The Italian landscape attracts this type of tourism (open-air tourism), as well as the themes of nature and naturalness. However, naturalness today is experiencing a critical historical moment, given that it is no longer just the picturesque that attracts people, but also an ethical naturalness, attentive to consumption, materials and habits that embrace the theme of sustainability. Consequently, the theme of the landscape and, specifically, the sustainability of open-air accommodation facilities has become a contingent theme that impacts the market. The interest in this type of holiday has started to involve different kinds of users, even those of a higher (economic) level, with a consequent change in the requests for the service.

The campsite, which, despite its historical evolution, still differs from the "tourist village" as a type of service, has had to adapt somehow to a specific request from tourists. Given the immanent link of this type of "tourism" to the natural context, its relationship with the issue of sustainability remains less evident than it may appear.

According to the WTO[10] Manila declaration, economical, sociocultural and ecological aspects characterise the impact of tourism. Five parameters define the ecological impact:

Pollution: air pollution related to car traffic – water pollution (sewage, waste discharge, solid hydrocarbon discharge from boats); waste pollution of tourist areas; noise pollution;

The loss of natural landscapes: the construction of buildings leads to the invasion of open spaces; some areas are closed to the public because private individuals purchased them; the construction of structures involves the disappearance of entire wooded areas;

The destruction of flora and fauna: the oversized influx of tourists can lead to the disappearance of some species;

Congestion: the concentration of tourists on holiday in a specific place causes damage to the landscape. The traffic congestion on the roads during the periods coinciding with the holidays increases pollution, wasted time and enormous fuel consumption and an increase in $C0_2$ emissions.

Lastly, *the World Tourism Code*[11] also states that: "tourism in Nature or ecotourism are recognized as forms of particular enrichment and enhancement, provided that they respect the natural heritage and local populations and respond to the welcoming capacity of places".

The phenomenon of "*overtourism*"[12], or "*tourist overcrowding*" is the impact of tourism on a destination, or parts of it, which excessively and negatively influences citizens' perceived quality of life and/or the quality of visitor experiences. The consequences related to the production of CO_2, waste generation and the generation of a temporary imbalance in a defined habitat have generated reflections on these structures' environmental impact, notoriously linked to open space and nature. It is, therefore, appropriate to understand that a mass phenomenon such as tourism, concentrated in a small, limited dimension, has a significant impact on the territory, both from an energy and environmental point of view and from a linguistic, aesthetic point of view. The theme of the natural that characterises open-air tourism is often read as an inalienable fact, intrinsic to the place and somehow immutable. However, contemporary sensitivity towards the landscape, and a growing ethical sense towards the climate crisis we are experiencing, entail a substantial reflection on the role and impact of open-air accommodation facilities.

Questions

Given what has been illustrated thus far, in terms of the size and presence of tourists, to give a correct vision of the phenomenon, following the reflections already mentioned by Tiziana Trillo, it is correct to read these places as "sui generis" urban sectors and study them as such. Like the city of tourism (Trillo, 2003), the intermittent city of open-air tourism is experiencing a moment of revolution linked to changes in the approach towards nature and market changes in the provision of services. It must be codified in order to be planned.

These settlement systems are only open for a defined period of the year but occupy the space and use the entire territory. The transience of this dwelling is linked to time, and time is the common feature of the housing systems used in these settlements: mobile when owned by the user or removable when owned by the structure.

Finally, if we look at the pattern of the campsites, in most cases, we find the absence of a typical design, of territorial planning and over time. It is easy to understand the reason for this situation if one remembers the origin of campsite, in its initial stages, as a way to inhabit nature using only systems owned by the tourist and therefore removed at the end of the holiday.

This set of reflections, which considers the relationship between time, tourism and landscape, leads us to ask some substantial questions that are the basis of this discussion:

Considering the system of open-air accommodation facilities as a transitive and temporary city that can be defined as an intermittent city, what can the design strategies for these kinds of spaces be?
Are there other examples of non-tourist settlement systems of this nature that can show how to relate to the landscape and housing units?
Can open-air accommodation facilities be testing grounds for other similar situations?

Maxi-Caravan

Before answering, a brief excursus is needed on an element that decisively characterises contemporary open-air accommodation facilities, namely the Maxi-Caravan.

The time factor in these structures is historically considered short and transitive. The invention of summer, linked to the theme of holidays and vacations, leads to the idea of a time bubble in which to "live" in a state other than everyday life. The transitivity of this experience is one of the factors that has always characterised its identity. From the days when Thomas Hiram Holding explored the English countryside in kayak and tent, tourist campsites represent a compromise between "wild nature" and "holiday comfort". However, with mass tourism, particularly after the Second World War, the "housing" methods associated with campsite tourism have become more complex than the simple tent. The use of the car, which led to the advent of caravans and campers in the 1950s and 1960s, contributed to enriching the complexity of the landscapes of the accommodation facilities, which had to be structured due to the multiplicity of requests.

However, the differentiation of utilities, combined with the tourism boom and the post-War economic boom, has led to the definition of less spartan ways of inhabiting nature than the tent. Therefore, the idea of the chalet and the bungalow became the means through which the landscape of open-air accommodation facilities met with architecture.

Much more than the buildings of the fixed structures (built on the edge of the settlement and, in any case, often concentrated in punctual intervals), it is, in fact, in these micro-architectures where the comparison with living in nature on vacation found opportunities for comparison. The topics of "vernacular architecture", "modern architecture" and of one's "relationship with the landscape" are central issues related to the design of these microstructures. However, relatively few "cultured" examples have seen a critical approach to these situations when compared to the number of open-air accommodation facilities realised. The designer usually focuses on architectural buildings (cabins or bungalows alone, for example) without considering the entire structure. Undoubtedly, however, within the panorama of campsites and tourist villages, the mini-house calls for a comparison with the almost vernacular landscape. However, when developed in a substantial way, the idea of the village easily risks recalling that of the urban suburb, if not of the slum.

Today, the aforementioned sensitivity towards the landscape, accompanied by uncomplicated protective legislation, imposes extra caution for these mini-objects. The bungalow, or the mini-house, has become, in most cases, unthinkable and unacceptable from a regulatory point of view, especially in contexts with a sensitive landscape, which is where campsite sites are located in most cases. The open-air tourism market is reacting to this situation by favouring the spread of a specific industrial product, the "Maxi-Caravan" or "mobile home". Maxi-Caravans are an industrial product that straddles the traditional housing dimension and the special dimension of moving vehicles. Caravan Holiday Home is the official name attributed to the Maxi-Caravan, defined as a transportable vehicle for leisure accommodation that does not meet the requirements for the construction and use of road vehicles, but which maintains the attribute of mobility and is intended for temporary or seasonal employment. Like campers and caravans, the Maxi-Caravan is equipped with wheels and is removable and transportable (albeit with specific conditions). This characteristic means the possibility of installation on free land (but within open-air accommodation facilities). The living space of about 40m^2 can accommodate up to six people. These essential characteristics also place it in a hybrid situation in terms of legislation, and consequently, two types of limitations are regulated concerning this product: transportability and habitability. To date, the law that indicates the sizing of mobile-home spaces is the European product standard EN 1647, elaborated by the federated body of UNI CUNA, the Technical Commission for Unification in the Motor Vehicle. Firstly, the standard specifies the housing requirements concerning the safety and health of people when they use Maxi-Caravans for holidays as a temporary or seasonal housing solution. Secondly, it also specifies the minimum dimensions (of the ceiling, doors and windows) inside the Maxi-Caravan, the illuminated area ratio required for each room, the classification by degrees of thermal insulation and heating and some essential construction details in the realisation of the roof and attic. Lastly, it also regulates the degrees of structural strength linked to the stability of the structure and the fire requisites. As we will see later, the Maxi-Caravan stands as a hybrid between a mobile housing situation and a stable/traditional one. In terms of transportability, however, the limits imposed are those of exceptional transport, which therefore determines maximum lengths of around 10m, maximum widths of about 4m and maximum heights from road level of around 4m. In some situations, it is possible to find mobile homes larger and with several levels or floors. Still, these are almost always handcrafted and non-industrial products that are no longer approved by the market system today.

The mobile home is not a recent invention; in other contexts, it has also been used for a long time as a permanent home. In the United States, for example, it is easy to find this type of housing being linked to poverty, especially in poor contexts, as the work of the *Rural Studio* clearly illustrates. The *20K project* that the Rural Studio has been carrying out for many years concerns the possibility of finding an alternative to "mobile homes". The objective of the Project is

> to provide an alternative to the only option currently available in a similar price range: a used manufactured (mobile) home. Mobile homes are not only manufactured out of state (and therefore not feeding back into the local economy) but they also will only degrade in value over time (rather than increase in value as well-maintained stick-built houses will) [13] … The "20K" label arose from the original price tag established in 2005 as the total price of a house that someone in the lowest income bracket (living on government assistance) could afford to make a mortgage payment on. The actual price has increased over time, but the name and the goal of designing homes that could be purchased by anyone, have remained the same.

In France, on the other hand, the mobile home has a particular association. Although it cannot be used as a real home, it is recognized as a "seasonal home" and inhabited only temporarily.

The "mobile home" or "mobile leisure residence" is defined as follows: "Habitable land vehicles which are intended for temporary or seasonal occupation for recreational use, which retain means of mobility which allow them to be moved by traction but which the highway code prohibits to drive".[14] We will elaborate on the regulatory issue later.

In Italy, the use of these products is strictly linked to open-air accommodation facilities, which hold the necessary regulatory permits and guarantee their use related to tourism (Berizzi and Trabattoni, 2019). They, therefore, appear as real "minimal homes", equipped with a specific outdoor space, but with the advantages of easy installation and removal, similarly to those of a caravan. Connections to the sewage or electricity network take place externally (as with caravans). This industrial product can be positioned instead of tents on free pitches, but its visual and physical impact is clearly different.

Again, the reference to "vernacular architecture" in the idea of a village is easily transferred to that of the residential suburb, depending on the scale factor. The positioning of the Maxi-Caravans, in relation to the protection of the landscape and, therefore, to reflections of density and space, is a practice that deserves professional attention. Yet, the installation of a Maxi-Caravan inside an open-air accommodation facility is not bound by the granting of a permit, as it falls within the category of "free building activity"; it is the host tourist complex that must have been previously authorised by an urban planning, building and landscaping point of view (if required)[15]. The consolidated text of the permit excludes the installation of Maxi-Caravans (which fall within the category of mobile homes according to the current law) in structures authorised by regulators of new constructions. Suppose they were to be positioned in the private field. In that case, they would have to adapt to Italian legislation regarding housing standards and the rules relating to energy efficiency, which would substantially change their characteristics and spatiality.

Temporariness

Temporariness is, therefore, the founding characteristic of mobile homes. They fit well in the context of the campsite because they are either entirely, or almost completely, removable without significant modification of the soil on which they reside. On the other hand, however, the examples demonstrate how these industrial products are used mechanistically and mathematically. Since, from a regulatory point of view, there is no need for a technician, the installation of the housing units is managed internally by the accommodation facilities. The housing unit is usually positioned to optimise the space according to its possible presence without considering the visual or landscape impact.

On the other hand, the installation of a series of housing units should involve a reflection on inhabiting nature, the construction of the landscape and the anthropic and aesthetic impact of this settlement system. There needs to be more attention paid to the empty space, not in terms of finishes, but rather a reflection on the value of the relational space between the units, understood as a human space of qualification of the settlement. This absence of planning combined with a normative emptiness relating to mobile homes requires a reflection on these settlements that starts again from the theme of temporary living and the value of empty space and the landscape.

The time of use of these spaces is complex. The tourist season is usually open from April (Easter) to October (although these times are expanding). The tourist experiences the structure even faster, over the duration of a weekend or a week. There is, however, a longer time to consider; the duration of the outdoor facility as a function for the housing units. The shelflife of the industrial product is approximately seven years. With this frequency, the accommodation facilities replace entire settlement portions, modifying the landscape. These timings define the built environment, which not only must be able to respond in the short term, but must also take into consideration the construction of the place and its periodic modification.

As mentioned, this research aims to interpret open-air accommodation facilities intended as temporary cities by placing them in a system including other examples of human settlements with similar characteristics. If time, landscape and architecture are the three common themes that accompany this reflection, time is the one that defines the structure of this discussion. This approach proposes three temporary settlement types according to their lives and experiences. If the need for open-air accommodation facilities is to be planned as urban settlements, albeit special ones, the comparison with similar case studies can highlight the value of the analysis of these structures, as well as show their potential when linked to temporary living as a function of the enhancement of the place and the landscape.

If the campsite is analysed as a planned temporary settlement system, the terms of comparison must be codified in order to narrow the margins of analysis:

- Planning of the settlement system
- The organisation of homogeneous cells
- The construction of an open spatial system (built/unbuilt relationship)
- The intentional or accidental relationship with the landscape
- Temporary planning

According to these lines of analysis, two areas of comparison have been identified to crown the report on campsites:

1. Settlement systems linked to events, the temporality of which goes from one month to six months. Two exemplary and unique cases were selected: the *Burning Man* festival and the *Kumbh Mela festival.* When considering the camping time, these examples refer to "a short time", which involves, as we will see, a particular relationship with the settlement system and the landscape.
2. Settlement systems designed to be temporary but not removed. This is the case with refugee camps. Specifically, reference will be made to the refugee camps designed by UNHCR on the African continent. This choice is determined by the fact that these settlements, very similar to informal slums, are actually created with precise

> planning linked to settlement times and housing units. This initiatory characteristic makes them an interesting term of comparison, especially in the final phase of the analysis. Considering the few experiences of refugee camps removed, we can assume that the lifespan of a camp varies from around 20 to 70 years and beyond (depending on the year of foundation). The accidental permanence of these settlements involves a reflection on living spaces and urban morphology in a context that is almost a city, but which can also take suggestions from the camping experience.

In these panoramas of housing situations linked to the community or that of an occasional community, the construction of space is connected to the language of the architecture of the housing cell. More than the collective, punctual and extraordinary elements, the housing cell becomes the matrix of the space. All the examples that will be proposed work with a low-density housing system (minimum housing unit) developed horizontally. The considerable downside is the lack of attention to the interstitial space between the housing cells. Therefore, the landscape's construction reflects the relationship between the units, according to the spaces of connection and the relationship with the natural element. According to these terms of comparison, the time of the accommodation facilities in the open-air is defined as average (with the methods indicated above) in relation to the other examples proposed.

Among the settlement systems we will analyse, physical, elemental and morphological similarities cross very different cultural contexts. Inhabiting the landscape, understood as an enhancement of the empty space and the natural context, is a qualifying design principle of these settlements.

In his *Ethics of Building the City*, Richard Sennet distinguishes the urban context in the built context (la Ville) and the social/human context (Citè). Ville and Citè chase each other in search of a balance between the formal and spatial definition with that of relationships and society (Sennett, 2018). In temporary living contexts, the relationship between space and relationships, form and function, significantly involves the natural context, generating unique landscape systems. The coherence between Ville and Citè is refined thanks to the time limitations, but it is not resolved precisely as a function of the third character of the play: the landscape. Therefore, the key to reading this manuscript is that of a duel between three voices, which, as Sergio

Leone[16] has shown, is a dynamic system that does not find a definitive solution, but opens up some potential scenarios.

We will introduce the short-term stay (quick time), discussing the immediate cities linked to periodic or univocal events. We will then move on to a slower pace (medium time), that of the holiday, speaking of open-air accommodation facilities with a particular focus on the reality in Italy, which is a representative example. Since this context is also the object of planning, graphical analyses and settlement strategies will be presented that respond to the needs expressed by the thesis. Finally, the long-term stay will be introduced (long time); that of the refugee camps designed and built by UNHCR. Applying settlement theories related to the campsite will then be proposed to verify their similarity and applicability.

Notes

1 AUDe is a research laboratory of the University of Pavia, Department of Civil Engineering and Architecture, which deals with architectural and urban planning – https://aude.unipv.it/.

2 https://aude.unipv.it/ricerca/mobile-homes-per-il-turismo-sostenibile/.

3 Crippaconcept is one of the main Italian producers of Maxi-Caravan – https://www.crippaconcept.com/#.

4 Trabattoni, L., Capotorto, M. and Berizzi, C., *Progettare lo spazio minimo delle maxi-caravan. Qualità, ergonomia e fruizione degli ambienti interni*, AUDe; Crippacampeggio srl, 2024, ISBN: 979221058345.

5 The information about this project is open source on the website of AUDe – https://aude.unipv.it/wonderland/.

6 www.campdesign.it.

7 FAITA – federazione italiana turismo all'aria aperta – Verso un osservatorio sul turismo all'aria aperta, dalla revisione delle statistiche alle indagini sulle imprese (FAITA – Italian Open Air Tourism Federation – Towards an observatory on open air tourism, from the review of statistics to business surveys), May 2023, p. 7.

8 https://ec.europa.eu/eurostat/en/web/products-eurostat-news/-/ddn-20210401-1.

9 "l'Osservatorio Turismo Outdoor | Previsioni Estate 2023", report created by Human Company and Thrends.

10 29 June 2017 UNWTO The Manila Conference set a roadmap for measuring sustainable tourism: nearly 1,000 experts from over 80 countries gathered for three days (21–23 June) in Manila, Philippines, to discuss sustainable tourism in its economic dimensions, social and environmental.

The resulting "Call for Action on Measuring Sustainable Tourism" is a complete, coherent and solid information base.

11 The World Code of Tourism Ethics, adopted by resolution by the General Assembly of the World Tourism Organization in Santiago de Chile (27 September–1 October 1999), has as its fundamental objective that of promoting responsible, sustainable and accessible tourism to everyone. The document was republished in Italian, with a new graphic design, in February 2010.

12 World Tourism Organization (UNWTO), Centre of Expertise Leisure, Tourism & Hospitality; NHTV Breda University of Applied Sciences; and NHL Stenden University of Applied Science, "'Overtourism'? Understanding and Managing Urban Tourism Growth beyond Perceptions: Executive Summary", UNWTO, Madrid, 2018, Available at https://www.e-unwto.org/doi/epdf/10.18111/9789284420070, p. 4, Accessed on 25 August 2020.

13 http://ruralstudio.org/2020-20k-home/.

14 "Décret n° 2007-18 du 5 janvier 2007 pris pour l'application de l'ordonnance n° 2005-1527 du 8 décembre 2005 relative au permis de construire et aux autorisations d'urbanisme) // Section IV, sous-section 2".

15 The Consolidated Building Act (Presidential Decree n.380 of 6 June 2001, Legislative Decree n. 222 of 25 November 2016) provides information relating to the subject of interest dealt with. Article 3 (Definition of existing buildings) in paragraph 1 e.5 specifies that for new construction interventions: e.5 "the installation of light products, even prefabricated, and of structures of any kind, such as caravans, campers, mobile homes, boats, which are used as homes, work environments, or as deposits, warehouses and the like, for with the exception of those intended to satisfy purely temporary needs or tents and mobile housing units with rotating mechanisms in operation, and their appurtenances and accessories, which are located, even on an ongoing basis, in outdoor accommodation facilities for parking and the stay of tourists previously authorized from an urban planning, building and, where applicable, landscape point of view, who do not have any connection of a permanent nature to the land and present the dimensional and technical-constructive characteristics envisaged by regional sector regulations, where existing".

16 In the famous film *The Good, the Bad and the Ugly*, the scene of the duel of three voices is resolved with a masterful direction shot in which the camera, passing from one face to the other of the protagonists, starts a dynamic rotary movement, which it follows and defines the space in a continuous acceleration up until the climax of the shot.

1 Prologue

An Introduction to Temporary Settlements and Living Landscape (Quick Time)

"Time" and "dwelling" are historical concepts related to architecture. As Anna Barbara reminds us, "the question of time before becoming a project is philosophical, existential and semantic" (Barbara, 2012, p. 5). However, if defined according to the territory and the landscape, time and dwelling immediately refer to well-known concepts linked to nomadism and dynamic and transitory use of the territory.

The most famous historically nomadic populations of the world, such as the Native Americans or the Tuaregs of the Sahara, followed a land use of necessity. The dynamic movement through points of water could be read as movements along natural service infrastructures: natural infrastructures determined by climatic conditions, the presence of water and the movement of animals. The human impact on the landscape was minimal, and the language of architecture was negligible in relation to the speed of use of the places and the use of domestic space. Native American villages, for example, are dynamic structures codified on the housing unit (teepee) and its aggregation.

The teepee consist of three elements: a set of poles, of which the number varies according to the size of the teepee (11 for a 3–4m tipi, 14 for a 5m tipi...); a canvas or a cover of skins; and rope and pegs are needed to tie down the poles and anchor the cover. The teepees are distinguished from other tents by two decisive innovations: the upper opening of the smoke flaps, which allow the inhabitant to cook and warm up with a lit fire, and the versatile cover, which allows for a solid but controlled circulation system of fresh air and smoke disposal in any weather. The types are designed to be easily assembled and disassembled according to the movements of the inhabitants, primarily to chase bison herds[1]. The *tipi* or *teepee* represents the

DOI: 10.4324/9781003468530-2

domestic dimension, is organised on the social relationships between men and women and identifies the cellular condition of the individual (or family), which creates the community by extension. Beyond the tribal rituals, which generate unusual uses for tents or the construction of ad-hoc tents, the settlement structure of the village remains identical and changeable. A set of points that adapts to the terrain without changing it.

The same can be said for the Tuareg villages. The Tuareg are a semi-nomadic ethnic group located along the Sahara Desert (mainly in Mali and Niger, but also in Algeria, Libya, Burkina Faso and even in Chad, where they are called Kinnin). Their tents are built during the wedding ceremony and metaphorically represent the extent of the union between the two individuals; they belong to the woman but are placed near the man's place of origin. The tent represents an essential symbol of the Tuareg nomadic cultural heritage. It is a central element within family and social relationships in Tuareg society. It is a single space where all the important activities of family life take place, from eating to sleeping. The tents rest over the desert; they do not change the terrain, which is, by nature, difficult to live on. The Tuaregs learnt how to build and pitch their tents from their ancestors. According to Tuareg beliefs, the north of the tent is considered harmful because evil beings called *kel-esuf*, "those of solitude" (Fisher, 2017), flock from that direction in large numbers, especially at dusk, while the south is laden with blessings.

A similar argument could also be made for the Mongolian yurts (ger). Also, in these cases, the housing unit, functionally developed to respond to the climate and accommodate traditional rituals, determines the settlement system. The construction of a "public" space does not exist. Instead, the housing unit is placed in the landscape close to other units, defining housing clusters where the void, the interstitial space between the houses, is nature itself.

In these cases, the village is the icon (Comi, 2009, p. 21)[2] of the image of the ideal city of the community. The city understood as a place appears as a timeless construct. Taking up Richard Sennet's dichotomy, the Ville represents the immanent image of the citè in an iconic and symbolic way. The set of housing units, the set of individuals, defines the space of the community. The relationship with the landscape, being temporary, is only one of necessity (water, sun, wind, food), and the modification of the landscape that inevitably derives from the mixture of artificial and extraneous elements to the context does not disturb the harmony of the gaze. Man's space is so small compared to what does not belong to him that it is not even defined as an enclosure, but only as a virtual pertinence. If traditional nomadism is difficult to modernise, the theme of quick time when applied to living has often been the subject of architectural reflection.

There are many examples of temporary houses, both temporary in use or duration, and transportable houses. Just consider the numerous examples of emergency and non-emergency houses, ranging from Buckminster Fuller's Dymaxion House to Renzo Piano's Diogene, to mention two examples known to all[3]. The theme of the temporary city, on the other hand, is understood as a settlement system and not a community (thus leaving out the reflections on the social nomadism of the "new poor" – la ville and not la citè) and is mainly linked to some city projects of the 1960s and 1970s. These examples refer to an urban dimension linked to the event, immediacy and transition.

The Archigram projects, expressed on Zoom and in *Archigram* (the magazine) through exhibitions and conferences, are the best-known examples of the development of an urban conception that sought to undermine a traditional approach by looking at a dynamic city from a futuristic point of view. The first visions proposed by Archigram concerned urban megastructures. The "*Plug-In City*" was influenced by the theories of Reyner Banham and by some important post-War projects, such as Mobile City (1957) by Yona Friedman, Floating City (1959) by Kiyonori Kikutake and Tokyo Bay (1961) by Kenzo Tange.

The *Plug-In City* intends the temporariness of living to be expressed through a dual-element system. The megastructure that expands unconditionally determines the possibility of the minimal housing units to be positioned at will along its development. In addition, this large facility supports infrastructure and plug-in housing components that can be swapped out as consumer needs change.

> Upon the publication of "A Home is not a House" in 1965, Archigram shifted their attention from the megastructure to the portable environment. This shift is evident in *Archigram 6* (1965), which featured pneumatic structures made by American companies for use as warehouses.
>
> (Deyong, 2017, p. 5)

The Walking City, designed by Richard Herron, is the transition from a static to a moving megastructure. It comprises several gigantic nomadic elements containing different urban and residential areas and resources. Connected by a superstructure of retractable corridors, they form an instantaneous, itinerant metropolis that walks and adapts to constant change.

> For Cedric Price, an architect who shares concerns with Archigram, the parts of the Walking City were living creatures that "roam the globe forming and reforming." There is a military quality to their tanklike structural vocabulary, described in Herron's strong graphic language, although no tank would have their skylightlike tension-skinned roofs.
>
> (McQuaid, 2002, p. 50)

Finally, it is in the *Instant City* that the approach to the temporary becomes effective. The city disappears, and becomes a system of communications and events, which seems to modify the context and then disappears. The architecture disappears, giving way to images, events, audiovisual presentations, gadgets and other environmental simulators. With the Instant City, the architects developed the idea of a "travelling metropolis", a package that temporarily infiltrates a community. This city superimposes, for a specific time, new communication spaces in an existing city. The Instant City is precisely what its name suggests: it is the place of the event and gives rise to an event, shifting the value of architecture from artefacts to the interaction of people.

In Archigram's projects, the landscape is accidental and disappears. The real landscape is the urban one built by the interaction between the units (even when megalithic), and in this way, it returns to being timeless in its transitivity. The *Instant City* is the apotheosis of this approach, so much so that even the city's physicality disappears, which is no longer made by architecture or landscape, but is based on relationships. However, the modern and contemporary city is not temporary, not in its physicality. Even if the times of living, linked to domestic and urban spaces, have changed over time, the city's space coincides with a physical place, immobile in its transitivity. Horizons and urban conformations change, but the seat of the city is immobile. Although *society* is now defined as liquid (Baumann, 2000) due to its transience and we recognise figures who inhabit it nomadically (Dagnino, 1996)[4], the physicality of the urban space and its immanence towards the territory remains an inalienable presupposition.

The topicality of the Archigram projects is found when dealing with "unusual" settlement systems. When the "city" topic, understood as a human settlement, is defined due to unique events, the city returns to being nomadic. In this case, hybrid housing paradigms are generated halfway between known and utopian models. The comparison with the place, the organisation of space and consumption management are issues that must be addressed according to the event. In addition, the morphological systems that underlie these "temporary cities" have particular planning. There are a few examples in which these settlement events are confronted by landscape and urban planning. To define this topic, we will deal in depth with two examples: the *Burning Man Festival* and the *Kumbh Mela.*

However, before considering these two topical cases, it is interesting to mention other situations where planning does not exist or is excessive, generating ambiguous but exemplary situations. For example, the tent city of Mina. Mina is a small town located within a low valley in the Makkah province of western Saudi Arabia, about 8km east of the holy city of Mecca. Initially, pilgrims brought their tents, which they would erect on the plains of Mina. At the conclusion of the Hajj[5], the tents would be taken down, and everything packed up and brought back. In the 1970s, the city and its valley were the subjects of a project for a temporary city for pilgrims to Mina, proposed by Kenzo Tagne and Kenji Ekuan in 1974.

> Embodied the oil embargo, faisal turns to Tange with a crucial commission. In a valley five kilometer of Mecca, tange works with Ekuan to plan a temporary city for two million pilgrims on the Haji each year. The 635-hectare valley is sacred ground and must be kept free of permanent structures, so tange and Ekuan design equipment – tents with sleeping bunks, shower, toilets, water tanks, garbage cans – that can be stored under platforms at the edge of the valley and rolled out every year for four days before going into hibernation again.
>
> (Koolhaas and Olbrich, 2011, p. 351)

The project intervened on a sensitive, sacred landscape, trying to limit the margin of occupation but reaffirming the presence of architecture. The artificial margins of the Pilgrim City, which represent the infrastructure serving the event, rectify the natural margins of the valley, translating the natural orography into an articulated system of volumes.

"The theme of the megastructure dear to metabolism is found in the few design visions that accompany the Pilgrim City, which never saw development due to the death of King Faisal" (Koolhaas and Olbrich, 2011, p. 351). Today there is a city of tents in Mina that has followed another development idea. In fact, since the 1990s, the Mina Valley has been covered by a city of permanent tents. Today, within the 20km^2 valley, tents cover every open space as far as the eye can see, neatly arranged, row after row. In these tents, pilgrims stay overnight during the five days of each Hajj season. However, for the rest of the year, Mina remains virtually deserted.

> Out of a total of 1 million pilgrims, the vast majority of 850,000 pilgrims come from abroad, while domestic pilgrims account for only 15% or 150,000 pilgrims; there are more than 100,000 air-conditioned tents in Mina providing temporary accommodation to 3 million pilgrims. The tents measure 8 meters by 8 meters and are constructed of Teflon coated fiberglass to ensure high fire resistance[6].
>
> (Maisah, 2022)[7]

The tents are organised into several camps, each with its own outer wall and connected to other camps by trails. Each camp is equipped with a kitchen, toilets and ablutions facilities. Each tent is colour-coded by country and numbered, and all *Haji* should have badges with their colour and number on them in case they get lost.

The paradox of the city of Mina exemplifies the difficulties associated with the temporality of the settlements: a temporary housing system, such as that of tents, which becomes a stable settlement system, but is used only temporarily by a visitor. In this dense agglomeration, the sacred landscape has disappeared, not only in its natural dimension, but also in its dimension of interstitial space. The city of tents fills every space, and since the activities are elsewhere, it develops like a dormitory city.

The two Everest base camps represent another interesting reflection on the temporary. Everest Base Camp refers to the structure from which mountaineering expeditions to Everest depart. In reality, there are two base camps on Everest: the first, on the southern slope (the Nepalese side), is located at an altitude of 5364m, at the foot of the Khumbu glacier; the second, on the northern slope (the Tibetan side), is located at 5154m at the foot of Rongbuk Glacier. The base camps are inhabited continuously, even if they are temporary situations. The spatial organisation is non-existent, as in an emerging camp, it is fixed on stable "tents" (for the necessary adjustment phase given the high altitude).

> Hundreds of hikers arrive at the two base camps (with appropriate and necessary permission), and not all of them continue.[8]

The presence of people, housing systems and necessities generates an urban-type situation in the complete absence of the public. However, the problems associated with human habitability remain, which makes it necessary to reflect on the settlement impact of this situation. As Freddie Wilkinson writes in *National Geographic*:

> At Nepal's Khumbu Glacier Base Camp, for example, the Sagarmatha Pollution Control Committee ensures compliance with health standards. Chinese officers play the same role at the Rongbok glacier base camp. The tents intended for services are built in such a way as to take away the sewage in plastic barrels coated up to lower altitudes, where it is disposed of. Garbage is handled in the same way. These practices ensure that modern camps remain relatively clean, but it only takes a little distance from the paths to find large piles of waste: what remains of shipments conducted in far less respectful times.
>
> (Wilkinson, 2020)

In this case, the complete absence of planning generates a continuous emergency housing situation embedded in the landscape. Like the bivouacs of the Italian Alpine areas, emergency shelters and protective shells for the night, the camps of Everest are positioned in the landscape. The constant influx of tourists, however, transforms this "uninhabitable" situation (so much so that the problem of biological adaptability to the altitude of the camps and the problems that this situation can cause is known) into a permanent situation that multiplies. Since there is no planning, there is no relationship with the landscape. In the massive emptiness of the mountain, the two base camps are accidental and accidentally final.

However, there are two cases in which the temporality linked to the settlement system has found an exciting solution. These are the experience of the *Burning Man Festival*, which is repeated every year in September in the Nevada desert for a month, and of the *Kumbh Mela*, the Hindu religious festival which, with its complex periodicity, occupies the flood areas of the Ganges and Yamuna.

The *Burning Man Festival*

The *Burning Man* is a festival created in 1986 and held annually in the Nevada desert. It is an event in which a community of people meets to shape a sort of temporary city called Black Rock City, which lives for only a few days, on the salt expanse (sabkha) of the Black Rock Desert in the state of Nevada, 90 miles (150km) north-northeast of Reno. Inside Black Rock City, the use of money is forbidden, bartering or donations are the only forms of exchange and complete self-sufficiency is required, bringing food, water and electricity so that it is not the urban infrastructure that has to compensate for the individual, but rather the community that supports the infrastructure.

Burning Man co-founder Larry Harvey wrote *Burning Man's 10 Principles* in 2004, and among them is the eighth, which is very similar to the world of sustainable design.

> Leaving No Trace: Our community respects the environment. We are committed to leaving no physical trace of our activities wherever we gather. We clean up after ourselves and endeavour, whenever possible, to leave such places in a better state than when we found them.
>
> (Harvey, 2004)

This implies excellent attention to the temporarily-occupied Nevada desert, where no traces, waste or residues should be left. The passage of the city and the community must not generate consequences for the landscape and the nature that hosts the community. The city thus seems to appear or rise in the desert, with a shape detached from the natural and strongly geometric, but then at the same time, the city later disappears as if it had never existed.

The morphology of the settlement is always the same. It has a central nucleus with services and primary activities and a semicircular system, with streets arranged radially concerning a concentric centre where the housing units are arranged. There is no study on the interstitial space between the housing units, but these define the shape of the city, organised according to passages; the streets are, in fact, the absent space between the units. Over the years, the sectors of the city have been codified, and today there is a thematic planning that distinguishes various areas:

- Plazas are located at 3:00, 4:30, 6:00, 7:30 & 9:00 on B + G Streets. These are mini civic centres and public gathering spaces with art installations encircled by creative and inviting theme camps and service camps. Emergency Services with first aid are located behind the plazas at 3:00+C and 9:00+C and Black Rock Ranger Outposts at 3:00+C and 9:00+C. Arctica ice sales are stationed at 3:00+G and 9:00+G plazas.
- Open camping is located throughout many blocks between H Street to K Street. Some of these blocks are open for unplaced groups to camp in, while others contain both open and reserved camping. Space for reserved, placed camps is marked on the playa with blue survey flags.
- Large area past K Street between 2:00 and 5:00 is reserved for walk-in camping. Camp without cars! No vehicles or R.V.s are allowed. You must leave your vehicle along K Street and carry your belongings to your chosen spot. The sheer difficulty of this exercise keeps Walk-In Camping sparsely populated, and your efforts will be rewarded with a sense of solitude unavailable in other parts of the city.
- Banks of porta-potties can be found throughout the city on radial streets on the blocks between C & D and G & H. The exceptions to this are 6:00, which has banks on D, and between H & I, and 3:00 and 9:00, which have banks on D and between G & H. There are also banks on the open playa on either side of the man along 3:00 and 9:00, and out by the Temple. There are some potty banks in deep playa as well. To help you find potties in your time of need, they are marked by solar-powered poles with blue lights.
- The Box Office is open 24 hours a day during the event and outside B.R.C.'s Main Gate.
- Center Camp is a vibrant hub in Black Rock City with an acre of beautifully designed, shaded, and welcoming space where all are welcome 24/7 during Event week.

Everything converges towards the centre, called "*playa*", where the formalised collective spaces reside (eating, dancing, meeting up, etc.)

and the actual meeting area, where the puppet is burned at the end of the festival.

The desert remains behind, looming in size but excluded from this urban planning that considers it only as a compensation of density: the void that opposes human aggregation. The surrounding landscape, flat and sandy, is the backdrop for this extraordinary temporary city. The constant threat of sandstorms results in the essential union between urban and landscape, making the connection between the two inevitable.

Regardless of the festival's ideological manifestos, the housing situation is an interesting reflection on the void: the absence of streets, squares and even the landscape (in the nullity of the desert, there are no facilities or points of reference) determines a housing condition where the outside is a space of occasional human relationships, while the codified ones take place in a defined fullness (the tent of services and aggregation). However, it is a situation with contradictions, as Paul Dobraszcyk explains.

> Its policy of cleaning up every speck of rubbish demonstrates ecological responsibility; yet, its annual centrepiece – the burning of ever-larger effigy of a man and many other structures – seems frankly distasteful in a world where climate change is stoking apocalyptic fires elsewhere. Its principle of inclusion is contradicted by the measure of control exerted on the funding of participating artists… .
>
> (Dobraszczyk, 2021, p. 39)

In the *Burning Man Festival*, it is easy to find one of the best examples of the Temporary Autonomous Zone (T.A.Z.) by Hakim Bey[9], those temporary community spaces outside the social and urban coding that seek absolute freedom of expression.

> the essence of the party: face to face, a group of humans synergize their efforts to realize silent desires, whether they are good food and happiness, dance, conversations, the arts of life.
>
> (Bey, 2007, p. 21)

The official website states that the festival is the city of citizens. The physical relationship with the built environment is not linked to living in the strict sense (the place of rest), but in a broad sense: living is expressing oneself.

> Burning Man is not a festival! Instead, it is a city wherein almost everything that happens is created entirely by its citizens, who actively participate in the experience.[10]

Therefore, we rediscover the Archigrams' idea of an event city, where Sennett's "ville" splits in two: on one side, the conglomerate of housing, a sort of infrastructure of necessity built on a geometric design imposed and coordinated from above. However, on the other side, a city built spontaneously coincides with the "*union of egoists*" (Bey, 2007, p. 21) that represents the citizens. The dual relationship between human/natural (artificial/organic) is developed complexly. A desire for alienation from the everyday, identifiable with the urban, in search of an exceptional nature, the desert, clearly materialises. The landscape, in this sense, is not chosen for its naturalistic/organic value, but for its opposition to the anthropic: the void.

Utopia can be built in a vacuum. In the void, it is possible to express one's freedom. However, to inhabit the void, the compromise of anthropisation is necessary, developed with an almost classicist order. All festival participants accept the concentric organisation as a pragmatic solution. There is no need to look for an organic form of (artificial) man's forms. However, a balance with nature is found through a quantitative operation: nature is everywhere because the desert is overwhelming. To touch it, to hear it, one just has to leave your shelter. The reference to the tribal dimension is obvious. Living in tents, the almost ritualistic constitution of events is linked to music and non-verbal communication, the almost sacred contact with the natural dimension. In its modernisation of the tribal, the festival introduces geometry and the need for organisation, and yields to the value of unity. This is understood as the minimum accommodation (even if the dimensions vary according to the occupant since the festival participants pay for the accommodation), and is organised by focusing on the collective.

It is clear that size matters. The *Burning Man Festival* hosts

> up to 66,000 people each year. In 2007, 47,366 people participated in the Burning Man Project; in 2013, the number of

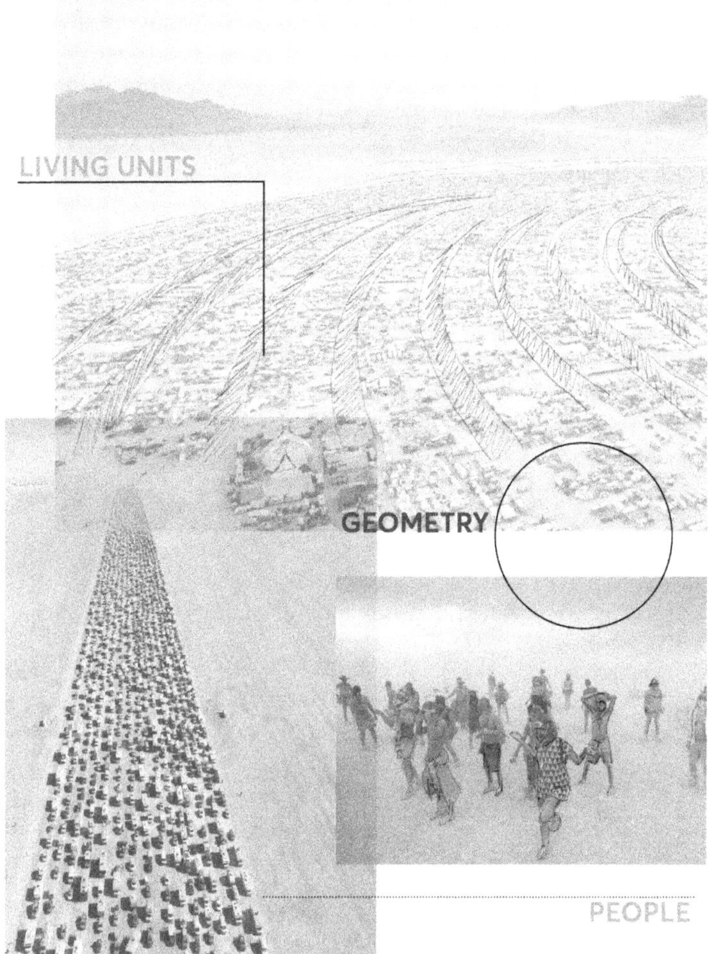

Figure 1.1 Black Rock City Collage

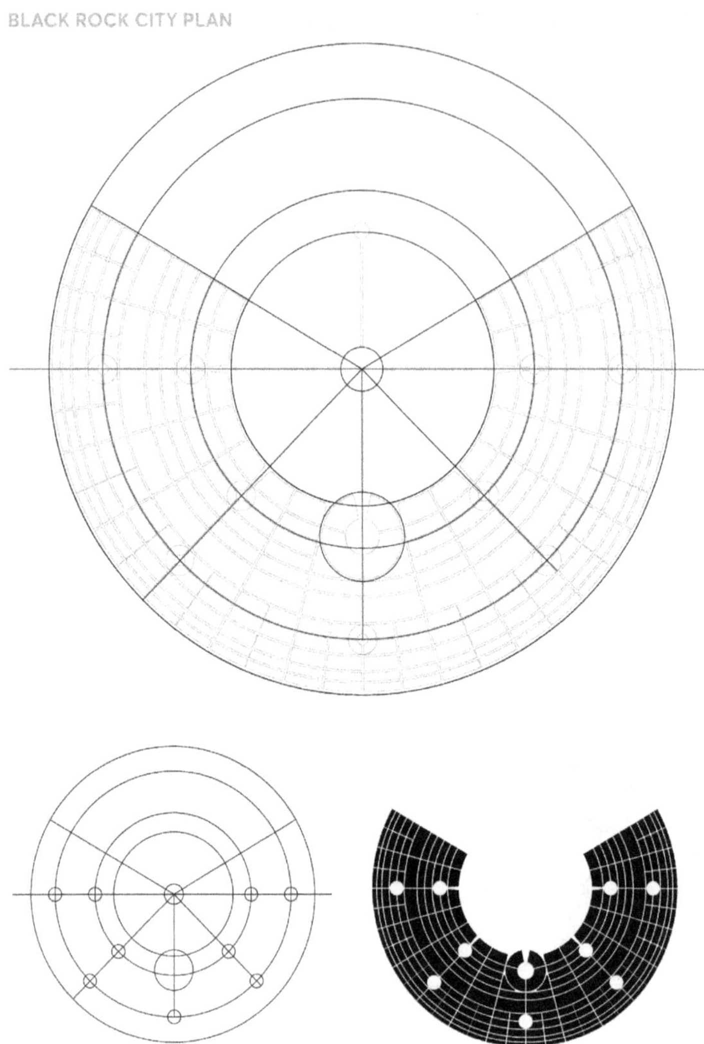

Figure 1.2 Black Rock City Diagrams

participants rose to 68,000 (currently the maximum number of participants imposed by the authorities), with a peak of 69,600 on the last day.

In 2014, due to bad weather that affected the first day of the festival and the greater control on the number of participants, having been exceeded the previous year, the number of participants reached the maximum of 66,000 people[11]. The dimensional ratio with a Sioux village is about 1 to 10. The tribal dimension, however, remains in an evocative form, linked precisely to the founding gesture of the festival, or rather the bonfire of the human puppet. However, unlike the Sioux village, urban planning is codified and controlled. It is therefore not surprising that the settlement system is also evocative, an immediate reference to the foundation cities such as Palmanova or the utopian cities of the late nineteenth century, such as the Victoria of J. Buckingham.

Geometry and size determine the urban landscape, which defines a habitable but uninhabited context. The inhabited context is instead that of nature, an extreme nature, the emptiness of the desert, where living is the theatrical act of self-expression. The images of the *Burning Man* tell of anthropic, human and artificial presences in an empty landscape. The figures as monads revolve around each other. However, they are not a community, perhaps rather a "*collective*", as Marcus Steinweg[12] defines it, a set of people united by a common purpose and perhaps by a common time.

Kumbh Mela

Kumbh Mela is a mass Hindu pilgrimage where the faithful gather to immerse themselves in a sacred river. There are three versions of *Kumbh Mela*: Maha (big) Kumbh Mela happens once every 144 years and is held only in Pragraaj (Allahabad); Purna (complete) Kumbh Mela takes place once every 12 years, and the event rotates between the host cities (Allahabad, Haridwar, Ujjain and Nasik); and Ardh (half) Kumbh Mela is held every six years in India and is held in two places: Haridwar and Prayagraj (Gupta, 2006, p. 330).

Some 60 million people attended the 2001 Purna Kumbh Mela, making the ritual the largest gathering ever held worldwide. According to some sources, about 100 million people participated in the Maha

Kumbh Mela in Allahabad in 2013, while according to others, the number was closer to 80 million.

At the time of writing, the last *Kumbh Mela* was held in Haridwar, Uttarakhand, in 2021, and over 150 million people were estimated to have attended the festival over its several-month span. After 55 days, the temporary city of *Kumbh Mela* was dismantled and disappeared. It is a pop-up megalopolis of roads, bridges and shelters temporarily built for the event and pilgrims, and is one of the most important examples of a temporary city.

The government fully funds the pilgrimage, and the 2016 Kumbh had a budget of US$428 million (Ujjain Smart City Proposal, 2016). The money was mainly spent on infrastructure to facilitate accessibility and use, especially related to tourism (both national and international). State urban planning is limited to the zoning of the areas and the construction of infrastructures. In contrast, the construction and management of the zoning areas are entrusted to individual associations or private individuals.

The first stage of the design is linked to the study of the river and its flood areas. Then, the development area of the urban sector is defined based on its size. The second design element is instead technical, and is the system of bridges that allows pilgrims to cross the river and use it. A dozen or more floating bridges define an infrastructure that crosses and negotiates with the prevailing landscape and the system of sacred rivers, while determining the urban development of the settlement.

A grid, more or less orthogonal to the bridges, is defined as the development matrix of the temporary constructions. The book *Mapping the Ephemeral MEGACITY KUMBHMELA* represents an in-depth report on the city's urban planning and management complexity. Just look at the numbers:

> area 1,936.56 hectares sectors 14 parking lots 99 police stations 30 state police personnel 12,461 central paramilitary personnel 40 cctv cameras 85 variable signboards 30 fire stations 30 length of roads laid 156 kilometers pontoon bridges 18 length of pipelines for water 550 kilometers water tap connections 20,000 active water tube wells 40 kilowatt hours of power consumed 30 megavolt amperes length of electricity lines 770 kilometers streetlights 22,000 private electrical connections 130,000 electrical substations 73 allopathic hospitals 14 homeopathic hospitals 12 ayurvedic hospitals

> 12 hospital beds 370 individual toilets 35,000 public toilets 340 trench patterns 7,500 non-conventional toilets 1,000 temporary bus stations 5 regional buses in operation 892 local buses in operation 3,608 pilgrims (estimated) 120,000,000 pilgrims in residence for fifty-five days (estimated) 5,000,000 train stations in operation 7 trains in operation 750 people lost during festival (estimated), 200,000.
>
> (Mehrotra and Vera, 2015, pp. 434, 435)

A real city of services was developed, with spaces for activities, sleeping, toilets and kitchens, and space for merchandising or the purchasing necessities of pilgrims, all defined according to Hindu rituals and religion. "Thus, Kumbh Mela combines the festivity of a festival and fair with the intention and devotion of a pilgrimage" (Saha and Khare, 2020, p. 29). The resulting infrastructure generates a series of activities complementary to the ritualistic ones (mainly undertaken in the water). Therefore, in addition to the spaces for "sacred" functions, other activities are developed, such as accommodation (from a 2016 *Kumbh Mela* census, around 467 hotels were found, of which 22 were non-starred hotels, 25 were hostels partly built by Madhya Pradesh State Tourism Development Co-operation Ltd and others were privately run; the actual mobility infrastructure, considering that out of a total of 563 km of city roads, 279.55 km of existing roads were upgraded to facilitate the movement of people and traffic (Ujjain Smart City Proposal, 2016); and the technical infrastructure, such as that linked to services and waste, taking into account that in 2016 there were almost 34,000 toilets made available during *Kumbh Mela* for sanitation purposes. In addition, widespread arrangements were made to collect nearly 2,000 tonnes of rubbish during the *Kumbh Mela* event.

> The accumulation of units converges in an endless texture of textiles, plastic, plywood and several other materials, each organized in a smart infrastructural grid that articulates roads, electricity and waste. The pavilions constructed along the main street of the Kumbh City have colourful gateways, decorated with flags, flashing lights and spinning fluorescent pinwheels. Halls are provided where hundreds of pilgrims may sit for the discourses of a famous teacher. Gurus sit with their disciples and interpret sacred

> texts. Yogis demonstrate their spiritual accomplishments. Popular singers and musical artists are invited to perform.
>
> (Saha and Khare, 2020, p. 29)

After the tents and temples have been dismantled, and the cameras are gone, the gridded city remains etched into the banks of the Ganges. Footprints of tents survive in the grey silt. Farmers use these remaining lines of the metropolis to grow wheat and rice. So we go from a densely populated tent city to a pastoral landscape.

The relationship with the landscape of this temporary city is fascinating in its ability to find a substantial balance with the void. The temporary city's space is the uninhabitable river flooding area. Even considering the high catastrophic potential of an event with so many people in the same place, the result remains that of an intermittent city, appearing out of necessity but capable of disappearing altogether. Despite the human impact of the event, and despite the actual and potential ecological impact, as is well expressed by the research project "Ephemeral Urbanism: cities in constant flux" presented at the Venice Biennale in 2016 by Rahul Mehrotra and Felipe Vera[13], where the impact of the urban settlement emerges mainly in the waste matter, organic and non-organic, that accompanies the *Kumbh Mela*, the city appears and disappears, modulating itself partly on the forms and constraints of the river landscape, partly occupying it, to live in it intensely without modifying it. This occupation occurs by replicating a homogeneous system; the ordered grid of bridges and roads is repeated every time, defining a sort of intermittent city that rests on the landscape and incorporates it without changing it. The technical needs of services, water and settlement time are balanced with the spiritual needs of landscape use, generating an integrated living context.

The infrastructure city that appears and disappears is a theme remarkably similar to the urban visions of Archigram. Furthermore, the idea of building a habitable context following natural limitations, but with the function of the spiritual, determines a complex artificial/natural relationship. The use of nature is ambivalent. On the one hand, a settlement is used as a spatial matrix. The river, almost like a prehistoric legacy, determines the line of stock of the urban agglomeration. The lines of development of the city follow, rationalising the line of the river, up to the confluence, given that the bank conditions the settlement margins; at the same time, however, the city develops independently of the river; it does not touch it but laps it while maintaining a liminal space of use, the beach. In this case, the river is like the prevailing landscape in tourist sites, or that landscape system that characterises the place (the sea, the lake, the mountains, the hills), but which is not directly habitable. On the other hand, the religious use of the river coincides, in a secular vision, with the use of the sea in summer holidays: it is the motif that determines the way of living, which characterises the landscape that is not only looked at, but also used in a parallel and other way of living.

The river represents the main public space, both symbolic and real. Obviously symbolic of the rituals that accompany the festival, but also real because, in line with the rituals, it is in the river that people who go to the *Kumbh Mela* meet. However, the city overlooks the river without encroaching on it. No floating buildings exist; the city rises on the river's banks and develops inside.

The orderly grid that determines the spaces that individuals use follows the shape of the river bed. However, collective activities other than the ritual bath occur inside the tents. A respectful distance between the human and the sacred inevitably accompanies the distance between the human and the natural. It is interesting to underline how the relationship with the landscape is used, but not admired. There is no need at the *Kumbh Mela* to look at the river, and on the contrary, the agglomeration of tents and pavilions defines a highly introverted settlement system. The activities occur inside the pavilions, or the river, not above or in front of them. This choice of use that determines the choice of settlement further establishes the detachment between man and landscape, finally defining a city that was born for the river, and which is built on the river, but which does not seek a dialogue with the river if not utilitarian. Floating bridges are the only moment of physical interaction between the "city" infrastructure and the "nature" infrastructure. On the other hand, to quote Sennett again, in the *Kumbh Mela*, the semantic relationship between the city and citizens is asynchronous with respect to the landscape. Citizens use nature as a primary function. The city is contingent, a satellite concerning the landscape from which one must quickly detach.

Figure 1.3 Kumbh Mela Collage

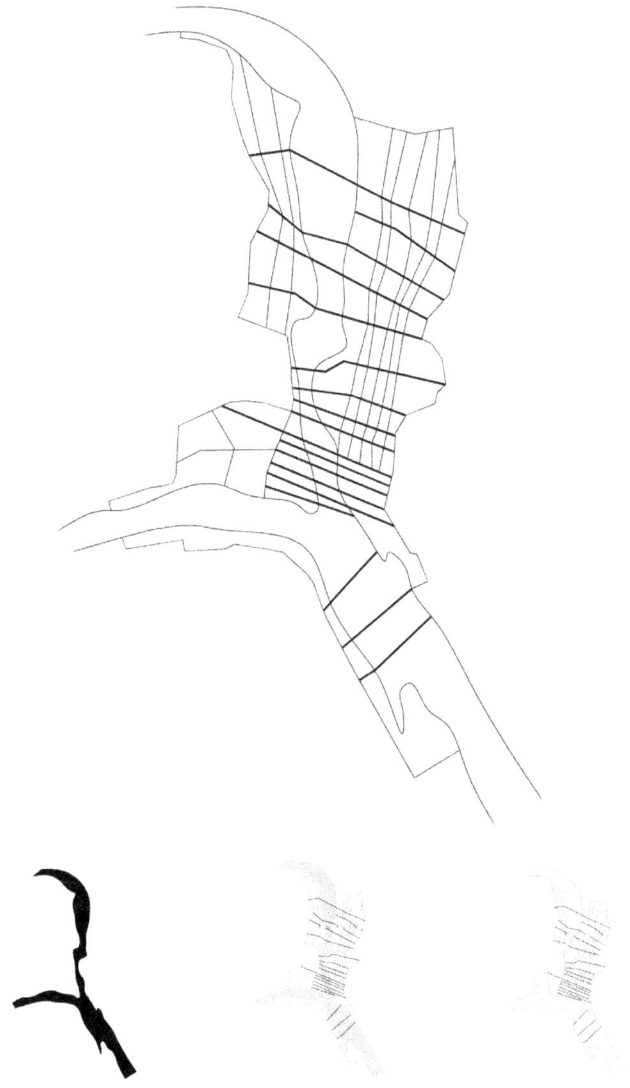

Figure 1.4 Kumbh Mela Diagrams

Quick Time

The temporary settlement systems that have been analysed present a different relationship with the landscape. The *Burning Man Festival* establishes itself independently, very reminiscent of the utopian cities of the nineteenth century. The urban form is synoptic of a social image. The balance with the landscape is determined by measure and necessity. The settlement size does not compete with the desert's vastness (both geographical and metaphysical). The forced geometry of *Burning Man* responds to the absolute emptiness of nature, not finding sensitive points of reference; it defines an autonomous ordered system. The complete removability of the city guarantees the balance. Emptiness remains empty. The artificial space built by man seeks identity in geometry, in pragmatism as a function of use. The main aggregation space is a void within a void (la playa), and the whole agglomeration is developed, tending towards this geometric centre.

The *Kumbh Mela* grows within the landscape by reading the territory more closely. The settlement rises in the flooded areas of the river, almost settling itself in a temporal and physical void, a space that disappears. The study of the flows of the Ganges and the Yumana is the first founding act in the urban planning of the festival. The city appears by reading the landscape, filling an uninhabitable space and connecting to other urban contexts. The theme of infrastructure is the founding theme. Nature is the main space to inhabit, while the city is a tool serving the relationship of man and nature. There is no search for a balance because the temporality of the intervention justifies the massive growth. However, on the other hand, the same temporality justifies an urban development of service, a sort of logistics space for the sacred. A direct comparison between the two examples described places them as illustrations of two opposing intervention strategies: the first, that of *Burning Man*, starts from the built environment, while the second, that of the *Kumbh Mela*, from the infrastructure.

The "urban" space of the *Burning Man Festival* appears thanks to the physicality of the built spaces. The private and collective tents are the only artificial element and, therefore, anomalous to the natural context of the desert. The size of the curtains and the relationship between them are the coordinates that lead to the definition of the final shape of the empty space, codified in a specific geometry. All other spatialities are the negative of the built. Therefore, the marked geometry of the settlement is a solution to give order to the system of points that defines the space. The metaphorical transposition on the social is evident. The relationship with the landscape is, therefore, accidental on the one hand (because it has no direct influence on the shape of the agglomeration), and decisive on the other, given that the formalism of the settlement appears as a physical response to the absence of reference in the desert void.

The urban space of the *Kumbh Mela* is the natural infrastructure, the river. Starting from this premise, it is unsurprising that the elements that shape the inhabited space are the infrastructures. The floating and removable bridges determine the main roads that intersect with the directionality of the river. This directionality is, in turn, replicated by secondary roads. This non-orthogonal grid outlines the shape of the space extending into the interstitial space defined by the river flood area: an expansion of the human realm within limits allowed by nature.

In both cities, there is a devotional relationship towards the natural element, which can be read as an empty habitable, non-designable space: The Ganges, where the natural baths take place, and the Nevada desert, which hosts the art exhibitions. Both of these voids represent a reference landscape, which determines the reasons for the settlement, but which remains detached from the settlement itself (although conditioning it in the ways we have just seen). In both these cases, the inhabited space (understood as space used by man) has a lower value in size and use than the "natural" one. The resulting landscape is therefore determined by the untouched presence of the prevailing landscape flanked by the extraordinary presence of human settlements. The short permanence duration of this situation is the reason that justifies the absence of interstitial spaces useful for the daily community, which in any case occurs regardless of the purpose of the pilgrimage. If the duration were "longer", the size of the event would become different, no longer just evocative, but almost touristic. However, tourism time is intermittent, while tourism space is stable. This dichotomy determines the relationship between these settlements and the landscape, especially if observed through the development of open-air tourism accommodation facilities.

Notes

1 Britannica, The Editors of Encyclopaedia, "tepee", *Encyclopedia Britannica*, 12 November 2018, https://www.britannica.com/technology/tepee. Accessed 2 June 2023.

2 According to Claudio Umberto Comi, in his book *Space, Time and City*, the icon is "… something that seems to us truer than truth because it brings together everything that seems plausible and true to us".

3 In this sense, see the historical list included in the book *Mobile Home*, an evolutionary story (Berizzi and Trabattoni, 2019).

4 Even more than a mosaic of wanderings in space, in fact, the current nomadism is a state of mind, an existential metaphor; it is the internalised awareness that reality is always transitory, in flux, that living will require a constant exercise of adaptation to increasingly different and ever more complex parameters. "Moving is no longer moving from one point to another on the earth's surface, but crossing universes of problems, lived worlds, landscapes of meaning. Today's nomadism mainly depends on the continuous and rapid transformation of landscapes, scientific, technical, economic, professional, mental... Even if we didn't move, the world would change around us. But we're on the move" (Pierre Levy) – Arianna Dagnino, *I Nuovi Nomadi. Pionieri della mutazione, culture evolutive, nuove professioni*, Roma, Castelvecchi, 1996. ISBN 88-86232-82-9 – p. 10.

5 "*Hajj*, also spelled *ḥadjdj* or *hadj*, in Islam, the pilgrimage to the holy city of Mecca in Saudi Arabia, which every adult Muslim must make at least once in his or her lifetime. The *hajj* is the fifth of the fundamental Muslim practices and institutions known as the Five Pillars of Islam. The pilgrimage rite begins on the 7th day of Dhū al-Ḥijjah (the last month of the Islamic year) and ends on the 12th day" (Britannica, The Editors of Encyclopaedia, "hajj", *Encyclopedia Britannica*, 15 February 2023. https://www.britannica.com/topic/hajj).

6 The current tents are the solution designed by the government to replace the previous tents and create a fire-safe situation, following a fire that occurred in 1997 that killed about 350 pilgrims. To prevent a repeat of the 1997 tragedy, a comprehensive fire safety network consisting of heat sensitive water sprinklers connected to an alarm system was implemented.

7 https://theislamicinformation.com/news/saudi-arabia-allocated-mina-camps-hajj-2022. Maisah – Maisah is a Muslimah and journalist for *The Islamic Information* based in Indonesia, studying law at Maritime University of Raja Ali Haji. She believes in the power of words and hopes that her articles will positively impact all of her readers.

8 According to Alan Arnette, a famous blogger who deals with Everest, in the spring of 2019, the Nepalese Ministry of Tourism granted 375 permits to climb to the top; on the north side, there were 144 foreign hikers.

9 Hakim Bey, *T.A.Z. La Zona Autonoma* Temporanea, Milano, Shake Edizioni, 1993, new edition Shake Edizioni, 2020, ISBN 9788897109822.

10 www.burningman.org.

11 *Burning Man Festival* draws peak crowd of 66,000 | SanDiegoUnionTribune.com
12 Marcus Steinweg – filosofo Tedesco – A collective, in my terms, is a community whose members are bound by nothing but the absence of an objective or absolute bond – "WHAT IS A COLLECTIVE?", 60th Lecture at the Gramsci Monument, The Bronx, NYC, 28th August 2013.
13 Venice Biennale 2016, "Ephemeral Urbanism: Cities in Constant Flux", curated by Rahul Mehrotra and Felipe Vera. Video by Henry Bauer and Cristian Pino Anguita, Available at https://www.youtube.com/watch?v=N8uu3VW_A48

2 Campsite Experience

Or the Dream of Walden Full Option (Medium Time)

It is difficult to give a temporal definition, in terms of duration, without making comparisons. Talking about short or medium, or long time may seem random. The short time of a city is in itself a paradox. On the other hand, the *Burning Man Festival* or the *Kumbh Mela* demonstrate the possibility of the existence of "removable" urban settlements. Their temporality is programmatic and immanent. Roberta Marcenaro defines the time of what she calls "mobile cities". These are transitory settlements linked mainly to emergencies, often with military management. Marcenaro describes three types of settlements about the length of stay: "the Initial city (less than a month), the Temporary city (6 to 24 months) the Semipermanent city (2 to 25 years)" (Marcenaro, 2011 p. 91).

Even the "city of tourism" (Trillo, 2003) is temporal, not in its physicality, but in its use. The idea of a city that we could define as "intermittent", which fills up in the high season and disappears in the low season, is a phenomenon encountered by many operators in the tourism sector. Users always use accommodation facilities temporarily, for short periods, even when they are open all year round. Outdoor tourism represents a unique case. In open-air tourism, contact with and presence within the open space are the foundations of the accommodation facility.

Different activities fall under the definition of outdoor tourism. The Italian panorama, for example, from a regulatory point of view, distinguishes tourist villages, campsites, agritourism and Alpine refuges[1].

Agritourism (i.e. the accommodation facilities that are integrated with structures with prevalent agricultural activities) and Alpine

DOI: 10.4324/9781003468530-3

refuges (which we could define as a particular category of high mountain hotels) are accommodation businesses that live off the natural landscape of reference, but which are organised as hotel businesses or similar and therefore can be open all year round.

Campsites and tourist villages, on the other hand, have a relationship that conditions the external space more, so their temporality is even more marked. We will see the difference between these two categories better later, which, although they have apparent differences, have many points in common as well. In this chapter, when we name "open-air accommodation facilities", we will specifically refer to campsites. These structures, by their nature, contain open space. With few exceptions, all the housing systems installed in the open space of campsites must be removable in order to leave the landscape in which they fit intact. Open-air accommodation facilities are characterised by the possibility of living in a protected landscape within one's own means (tents, caravans, trailers) or with "light" means provided by the accommodation facility itself (bungalows, Maxi-Caravans). The modality of use of these places involves a particular temporality, which can be balanced on two timings.

The first is seasonal. The opening times of open-air accommodation facilities vary from five to seven months a year (in hot countries). In Italy, where mainly this type of tourism is developed, campsites and tourist villages remain open from April/May to September/October. They are, therefore, habitable sites that only exist for a maximum of half of the year, which are discovered during the holding season and then closed. When they are closed while remaining active for maintenance and management, they are, in fact, inaccessible voids.

The second timing that affects these structures is linked to a specific housing typology: the Maxi-Caravan or mobile home. As we have seen, the housing typologies within a campsite can be of two different types. The housing systems provided by the outdoor facility itself are installed on specific empty spaces called pitches, sometimes equipped with the possibility of accessing electricity, usually grassy or with natural floorings such as gravel or earth. The pitches are organised by quantity and equipped with standard services (bathrooms, showers, laundries and more) created as permanent, stable buildings. The housing units traditionally provided by the open-air accommodation facility are the "bungalows". These small lodgings contain everything one would expect from a house, even if in miniature, and are built like ordinary buildings, and so are defined as permanent.

In Italy today, all campsites located in landscape-sensitive areas (almost all) have practically exhausted the possibility of building ordinary-type buildings, like bungalows[2]. An alternative solution was therefore developed for domestic-like accommodation provided by the accommodation facility: the Maxi-Caravan or mobile home. This industrial product replaces bungalows because it fits market needs and landscape protection legislation better. The Maxi-Caravan is a house of approximately $40m^2$ that is balanced to accommodate four to six people. It is supplied with a special cart (called a "chassis") that rests on the ground, is entirely removable and can be installed without foundations or particular ground precautions. It is, in fact, an object that can be placed anywhere inside open-air accommodation facilities (Berizzi and Trabattoni, 2019). Being an industrial product, however, it performs differently when compared to stable buildings in terms of spatiality, efficiency and durability. The estimated average duration of these mini-houses varies, usually between six and seven years.

The mobile home is, therefore, a vital element of the landscape of open-air structures, which, while maintaining the prevalence of empty spaces, can be equipped with large similar residential areas. Suppose the relationship with the landscape topic is a foundational theme of open-air accommodation structures. In that case, one can easily understand the importance of studying Maxi-Caravans, which become the only expressly anthropic element in a context that is empty and natural.

On the other hand, open-air tourism has an ambivalent relationship with the landscape. It thrives on the presence of a prevailing landscape that is made up of the prevalent landscape systems (the sea, the mountains, the lake), and which is not inhabited by structures but is used by tourists; to this landscape, the accommodation facility responds with an internal landscape, clearly anthropised, but at the same time aimed at enhancing the natural element. These places must maintain the prevalence of open space and must build this space according to the needs of the structure and the tourist.

Mobile homes fit into this panorama by raising some questions about living with nature, both from the point of view of language and landscape elements and environmental impact. Automatically, whether it is the object of planning and design or if it takes place in an artisanal and uncoordinated way, the internal landscape of the campsite is modified by the presence of the mobile home, just as any human settlement modifies the natural landscape. Naturally, this modification affects the terms of the architectural language. In addition, however, the furnishing and service elements of the public space (verandas, lights, paths, specific vegetation and use of water) are some of the elements that contribute to making the open space of the pitch more complex, usually settled with grass (or similar) and trees.

However, this "revolution" of the internal landscape responds to the timing of the industrial product, which changes with technology, size and customisation. Therefore, the average time spent in open-air accommodation facilities is complex. The form that responds to this complex time seeks to integrate the needs of the primary user, the tourist, with those of the accommodation facility and the landscape. The topic of sustainability is added to this equation, which, from a technical approach, asks to be aestheticised and conveyed. In this sense, the "natural" consolidates its relationship with the building.

Open-air accommodation facilities concentrate the study of open space on the ternary relationship between man, home and landscape. The first is a direct user, the second is an incisive element that defines a built context (albeit with its characteristics) and the third is a natural context, whose identity is defined according to its use. Nature remains the foundational element of these structures, not as an unchanged pre-existence, but in a more metaphorical and controlled way. In this way, the construction of the landscape of the open-air accommodation facility is a process that must take into account, in addition to the use of space according to the accommodation context, the aesthetic and functional relationship with the prevailing landscape according to the time of use, finally considering factors of revolution linked to the timing of the industrial product.

Defining the cultural panorama linked to open-air tourism is essential before considering the merits of the strategic/planning issues. The history of outdoor tourism is linked to some cultural revolutions related to a change of trend in reading the natural context and changes and advances within the world of work, such as the invention of paid holidays. Some pioneering experiences will then be illustrated.

There is, the first context that is defined by a series of experiences related to the "modern" holiday, or since the holiday and travel experience has become a mass phenomenon. The idea of providing an experience linked to living in nature declined in mass tourism. This is the case with *the English Holiday Camps* and some tourist planning, such as the *Costa Smeralda*, in Sardinia[3]. These examples show the attempt to codify a holiday system designed to live in open space and nature as a counterpart to everyday urban life. They are visions of "community", in which the group, the relationships and the management of the spaces define an almost dreamlike or utopian dimension.

The architectural context will then be introduced. Compared to the number of open-air accommodation facilities, relatively few signature projects explicitly address this issue. The sources that have been analysed are disparate and, in some cases, mainly graphic (as in the case of Albert Frey's Desert Hill Resort). However, certain conclusions were drawn regarding the settlement system and the relationship between buildings and the landscape. The design approach linked to campsites has always been zoning and agglomeration. Moreover, this is how they have been treated, generating spaces built for incoherent aggregations without planning or landscape protection.

Finally, there is a regulatory and definitional context linked to the landscape. Without going into the merits of the complex definition of what "landscape" is, we will proceed to list and illustrate the main definitions of the landscape from a cultural and regulatory point of view, taking into consideration the European countries that most confront the theme of campsite and open-air tourism in general.

Ultimately, we will proceed to illustrate a graphic apparatus of redesigns of Italian campsites to highlight, from a settlement point of view, the impact of tourism on the territory and the extent of these places. The urban dimension that will emerge will be the object of the final reflections of this chapter.

There is one last important note to make. Speaking of urban settlements concerning the natural context, a reference to the "great urban plans" of the 20th century and the "utopian cities" of the late-19th century is inevitable. This reflection has already been skillfully expressed in other contexts[4]. The parallel with the urban contexts is significant in consolidating the diachronic relationship between nature and the city, understood as antithetical. The escape from the city or the denial of the urban conformation as a function of new settlements or new ways of inhabiting space is the basis of numerous rethinkings of human living with well-known results, among the best-known examples of which is Eric Owen Moss' Garden City. Today nature and city find a point of conjunction, albeit with difficulty, in the theme of sustainability, which makes the former a technical solution that is applicable to the latter. From this point of view, open-air accommodation facilities can be studied as urban laboratories, where the natural theme is codified in its organic elements and anthropic translations.

However, there are substantial differences between the urban planning examples cited and the open-air tourism facilities, like the relationship between services and residential, and between public and private. The first is unbalanced, in open-air accommodation facilities, in relation to the living space, even if developed as a usable void. The second relationship is absent per se, but a translation of it can be found in the relationship between the collective and the unitary.

The difference in scale makes these constitutional gaps even more pronounced, making the two models challenging to match. The time factor, decisive in interpreting open-air accommodation facilities, acts differently in urban contexts. All utopian visions or large urban plans were conceived as replacements for an existing model, modifying its "Ville" according to the "Citè" (Sennett, 2018), but without compromising its temporality. Therefore, although there are cultural affinities, the urban examples of the late-19th and early-20th centuries that treated the foundation city as a function of a rediscovered relationship with nature, with health and aesthetic purposes, will not be considered. Nevertheless, they remain an underlying cultural reference linked to a particular way of seeing the space of man linked to nature.

ACT 1: HISTORICAL BACKGROUND

Trying to determine the genesis of the campsite phenomenon takes work. If campsite as a settlement act linked to leisure time can be traced back to some specific figures, its confirmation as a mass phenomenon needs to be clearer. The inevitable distinctions between the various European and non-European states generate a certain non-definition in the clarity of the phenomena that have contributed to the development of campsite as we know it today.

The change of perspective towards the natural element, the constitution of working holidays, the experiences of Thomas Holding, and William Murray, the development of infrastructures and the idea of travelling with tourist guides, the development of road and railway networks and the development of some technical inventions such as campers and caravans, are all fragments of historical background of the campsite. In the early 1950s, this panorama led to a mass phenomenon linked to the rediscovery of nature as a holiday resort and to the development of some pioneering projects that we will see in detail. First, let us clarify the pieces of the puzzle that define the cultural background underlying the examples we will illustrate below.

The birth of the campsite as a tourist phenomenon is linked to the rediscovery of nature that took place at the end of the 19th century. In that period, the consequences of the industrial revolution generated, among other things, a strengthening of the city/nature dichotomy in an antagonistic sense. Dickens' smoky London is the physical image of the society from which Thoreau's Walden flees, which seeks a positive value of rebirth in nature.

> I went into the woods because I wanted to live wisely, facing only the essential facts of life, to see if I could fail to learn what it had to teach me and not have to discover when I died that I hadn't lived. The thing is, I didn't want to live what wasn't a life unless it was absolutely necessary[5].

Nature goes from being a dangerous place to a place of salvation, both conceptual and real. In this sense, for example, the approach to the sea is emblematic, as told by Daniela Blei, as it passes "from being a source of food and where journeys began and ended, to a site of amusement and recreation" (Blei, 2016).

As Ana Swanson tells in the *Washington Post*, the medical needs linked to the discoveries of the time led to a different use of natural elements, which also led to a mutation of the landscape. The medical theories concerning melancholy, specifically those relating to the spleen and the theory of the *four humours*, later taken up by Robert Burton[6], proposed bathing in seawater as a treatment method. Similarly, Alain Corbin explains that "the discovery of oxygen by Antoine Lavoisier in 1778 led to the widespread diffusion of popular theories on the health benefits of sea air, which was thought to be more oxygenated and purer"[7]. "Wild" nature no longer represents a distant landscape, but becomes a place to consume and live. Think again of the sea and its transformation into a healthy place:

> The modern embrace of the beach for the purposes of health and hedonism, recreation and retreat, came with the rise of urban, industrial society. The European "discovery" of the beach is a reminder that human ideas about nature have changed over time, with real consequences for the environment and the world.
>
> (Blei, 2016)

Travelling in Nature

In parallel, the discovery of nature as a place to be admired goes hand in hand with the evolution and improvement of roads and transport systems. As Marc Desportes explains, the evolution of France's road layout is linked to the need for technical improvements in transport and a specific conception of the landscape. The Enlightenment approach of the "*strada dei lumi*" (Desportes, 2008, p. 75)[8] is similar to the rational approach of French gardens. In those years, the roads passed from having local management and maintenance to national supervision. The *Bureau de Pont*, managed by engineers and cartographers, redesigned the French road infrastructure, defining hierarchies and qualifying the roads according to rationality. At the same time, the evolution of means of transport was also advancing. The carriages became more comfortable, and the time spent travelling passed from a technical moment of necessity to a pleasant one. In this transition, those who travel look at nature and discover the landscape. The word "landscape" transitioned from a definition of a pictorial genre to a definition of a natural context (Desportes, 2008, p. 50). A general idea of rediscovered nature followed, echoed in painting and again in the architecture of gardens, which began to favour the English and oriental style, less tied to the aesthetic order than the classical ones. By making travelling on ordinary roads pleasant, travel became a moment of quality for everyone, and not just an elitist privilege, as was the case with the grand tour.

Until the end of the 19th century, the experience of the real journey, far from one's own country and in contact with nature, was an occasion for the privileged few. The Grand Tour was a long journey in continental Europe undertaken by the wealthy European aristocracy beginning in the 18th century and intended to perfect their knowledge through the journey. The term tourism and, more generally, the phenomenon of tourist travel today as a mass culture partly originated from the Grand Tour[9].

One of the characteristics of the first instances of mass tourism involved group travel, usually organised by subjects operating in the tourism sector. This form of tourism began to develop in the second half of the 19th century in the United Kingdom, and its most famous pioneer is Thomas Cook (Ingle, 1991)[10]. Thanks to the rapidly expanding railway network in England and Europe, Cook founded a company that offered ordinary people the possibility of affordable excursions, day trips and longer holidays in mainland Europe, India, Asia and the Southern hemisphere. In 1890 over 20,000 tourists a year travelled with Thomas Cook & Son (Sezgin and Yolal, 2012, pp. 73–74).

The theme of campsite intended as a rediscovery of nature in response to the conditions of everyday urban life has two founding fathers on both sides of the ocean: Thomas Holding and William Murray. Thomas Hiram Holding was an English tailor who explored nature with a tent and kayak in his spare time. In July 1897, aged 52, he designed and built a tiny, light tent that could be carried on a bicycle and set out on a three-day campsite bicycle tour of southwest Ireland with his son and two friends. In December of that year, he wrote *Cycle and Camp*, describing the trip in detail and praising the merits of nature travel and the affordability of that type of vacation. In 1901, T.M. Holding was among the founders of the first camper association: the Association of Cycle Campers. His travel reports were important documents for affirming the value of that type of travel, linked to this new way of experiencing the "landscape"[11].

William Henry Harrison Murray was born in 1840 in New England. He was a minister and served in a succession of increasingly prosperous and prestigious churches in Connecticut and Massachusetts. "During these years, Murray earned a reputation as a church leader and an eloquent, engaging speaker. However, he also gained notoriety for enjoying such outdoor recreations as hunting and fishing". (Young, 2018a). In 1869 he published a book named *Adventures in the Wilderness. Or, Camp-Life in the Adirondacks*, considered America's first "how-to" camping guidebook.

Murray's approach to nature is almost religious, but the book's success demonstrates the validity of its arguments. The stampede of visitors, which continued unabated through the summers of 1869 and 1870, came to be called "Murray's Rush", and its instigator gained a nickname:

> "Adirondack" Murray ... Yearning for a sense of belonging and connection, they heard Murray's call to the wild. The minister explicitly blamed urban life for his readers' yearnings and aches and prescribed campsite as a cure. Adventures, he declared, were written for those "who put up in narrow offices and narrower studies, weary of the city's din, long for a breath of mountain air and the free life by field and flood".
>
> (Young, 2018a)[12]

In France, the first literature on campsite dates back to 1898: a famous French camper and traveller, Lucien Baudry de Saunier, published an article in the Touring Club de France magazine that recounted his trip to England where he met English aristocrats using trailers pulled by horses or using the first carriages to move around their immense properties. The word campsite appeared in 1903 in the sports newspaper *L'Auto*, which mentioned the sports fields of the English who grouped themselves into the first campsite association in history, the Association of Cycle Campers. The campsite arrived in Italy in 1932 with the ACCP (AutoCampsite Club Piedmont), resulting in 1950 in the Federcampeggio. The first campsite in Italy was inaugurated in the Piedmontese capital, Turin, in the Parco Leopardi area. The characteristics that distinguished it were the presence of services, surveillance and payment for entry.

Vehicles

The advancement of technology linked to the means of locomotion and movement is another crucial coordinate related to the theme of outdoor holidays. Campers and caravans have become iconic outdoor facilities, in the same way as tents. Again, it is not easy to define the exact chronology of the genesis of the camper, and it may not even be necessary. There were several pioneering projects, all resulting from a prototype development that never became mass distributed.

One of the most famous examples of a camper designed for living while travelling for recreational purposes is the "*Bourlinguette*" by Jules Secretat[13], who had it built to order by the engineer Lafitte in 1903. Another interesting example is the "*Gypsy Van*" made in 1915 by Roland Conklin's Gas-Electric Motor Bus Company:

> A 25-foot-long, 8-ton camper that Conklin and his family took on a westward drive from Huntington, New York to San Francisco, California. It featured working electricity, lighting, a kitchen, appliances, and a roof garden. Visually arresting and cleverly designed, the 25-foot, 8-ton conveyance had been custom-built by Roland Conklin's Gas-Electric Motor Bus Company to provide maximum comfort while roughing it on the road to San Francisco.
>
> (Young, 2018b)[14]

After this year, the recreation vehicle market (RV) grew fast.

In the 1950s, the first camper models designed for mass production in Europe and overseas were produced in conjunction with the spread of mass open-air tourism. In France in 1951, a specialised press appeared and reported on two motorhome models, one by the firm "Notin" and the other as "Passe-partout" by Pierre Digue, both on a Renault 1000kg chassis. In 1961 the Italian company Arca produced the Noè model, which became a point of reference in the production of motorhomes in Italy. Also, in those years, the Volkswagen company, in collaboration with the Westfalia company, produced the T2 Combi model, which has become iconic of the hippie culture.

The ancestor of the camper is the caravan, whose invention dates back to 1885 in England by Gordon Stables, who, through a company specialising in railway construction (carriages), had a six-seater horse-drawn caravan built. Inside the carriage was a kitchen, table and sofa bed. Also, in this case, it was necessary to wait until the 1930s to reach mass production. The first modern caravan, linked to the car and designed for mass tourism, is probably the Wonhwagen, produced in 1936 by the Dethleffs company. Entrepreneur *Arist Dethleffs,* a salesman for whips and ski poles, did not want to do without the presence of his family on his business trips throughout Germany and so designed a mobile studio with sleeping accommodations for his wife and their daughter. The vehicle was designed with three beds, one axle and two wheels with tyres. It was 4,380m long, 1,660m wide and 2,050m high. The interior featured a bench that folded into a double bed, a table, a bunk bed and various shelves.

This roundup of examples is intended to highlight how much the type of open-air holiday has spread more and more over time.

Holiday Camp

Among the examples that clarify the evolution of the holiday linked to nature, it is also essential to mention the experience of the English "*holiday villages*". The "holiday camps", as they were called at the beginning of the 20th century, were a unique experience, and in their foundational characteristics, linked to the desire to provide a service to an extended public.

If the idea of an organised summer camp was already present in the United States at the end of the 19th century, it was intended for children in order to keep them away from the polluted climate of industrial cities (think, for example, of scouting). However, in England, this service has been developed for adults as a service for urban workers. Escape from the city to the coast and nature was a established habit, but a privilege of those who could afford it, who found refuge in hotels or guest houses. For the poorer classes, alternative and seasonal jobs were an alternative to the city. An example of this is the Hoppers, the hop pickers. The annual appointment linked to agricultural seasonality involved the movement of an ingenious mass of people who aggregated in temporary villages, generating a mobile community with its own timing and rituals. Working in nature was an essential and healthy alternative to urban work. The holiday camps were born in this context to formalise this popular need.

It is no coincidence that some of the camps were managed by workers' associations, such as the Derbyshire Miners' Holiday Center, which opened in 1939 for the miners of Derbyshire: "A week at the camp means good food and fresh air for workers who knows only dust and darkness for most of the year…" (Ward and Hardy, 1998, p. 69). However, most camps were family-run, especially those built between the two wars. The first, and perhaps one of the most famous, examples of these is the Cunningham Holiday Camp Douglas, built on the Isle of Man. Mr and Mrs Cunningham managed it for young men from Birmingham at the end of the 19th century; it initially consisted of a system of accommodation in fixed tents. The other camps later took up the idea of providing a "fixed price" holiday. The Cunninghams initially opened their camp to young men only, with the holiday including room and board and various activities.

The evolution of the Cunningham Holiday Camp over the years is also paradigmatic of the other camps that developed subsequently. Initially, with an accommodation system based on fixed tents (lodges), it was transformed into a prisoner camp during the First World War and a training camp for the Royal Navy during the Second World War. The tents were supplemented with bungalows. In addition, an indoor swimming pool, a ballroom and an open-air amphitheatre were built. At the basis of the stay was the idea of a shared holiday, with organised activities and equipment at the service of the holidaymakers. There was also an internal newspaper as if to underline the "community" nature sought by the camp.

Even if the Cunningham Holiday Camp has the primacy of timing, many camps were developed at the beginning of the century and between the two wars, and repeated the formula of the organised holiday.

> Pioneers camps were sometimes simply family ventures, modest in scale and offering plenty of fun at reasonable charges. In other instances, camps were sponsored by organisations for their member. They too were offering relaxing holidays in convivial surroundings, though sometimes with a dose of education and self-improvement to enrichen the experience.
>
> (Ward and Hardy, 1998, p. 48)

These "pioneers" were mixed and and examples of family camps were the Harsen't Camp in Pensarn in north Wales, the camp in Otley Chevin on the Yorkshire Moors, the Potter's Camp at Hemsby in Norfolk and the famous Caister-on-Sea, on the East Coast, opened by J. Fletcher Dodd in 1906 and known as "*Caister Socialist Holiday Camp*". The accommodation for the latter was in tents, and the campers helped out with the chores. After the First World War, chalets and huts replaced the tents in order to accommodate 800 persons. The camp also had a licensed bar and provided organised games, sports and trips to the Norfolk Broads. It was situated on the beach and had over 90 acres of land. Another example was the

Golden Sands at Voryd, Rhyl: "It was started in 1933 by Arthur Jones, formerly of the merchant navy, who had a timber yard in the town. It had both one-room chalets and tents and a vast pavilion, built entirely of wood, for dining and entertainment" (Ward and Hardy, 1998, p. 54).

Braggs and Harris (2006) and Ward and Hardy (1998) explain that it is possible to distinguish the evolutionary path of holiday camps into two phases. The initial phase, which starts with the Cunningham Holiday Camp, is called the "pioneers". It is characterised as mainly family managed. The offer is concentrated on shared activities in the middle of nature. The dimensions of these structures are small and contain spaces both for tents and chalets. The idea, codified in retrospect, is that the maximum size of people in the camp is 500; "beyond that number ... it was not possible for a very rich and corporate life to be enjoyed by the campers" (Bragg and Harris, 2006, p. 116). The second phase is the one following the Second World War.

It is interesting to note that many camps were used during the war for military purposes, both as prison camps and as military and training bases. This contingency in some cases favoured the maintenance of the camps, which at the end of the war were already ready to be used again.

A figure of note from this era is undoubtedly that of Henry Butlin, who, more than any others, managed to channel the requests of an ever more extensive and more varied population. The Butlin's camps were codified less in the structures than in the service rendered: the organised activities, the morning wake-up call, the redcoats (orderlies, helpers, handymen), the shows and the guests. According to Ward and Hardy, the Butlin's Holiday Camp represents an effervescent climate of post-war growth.

Post-War summer camps, such as those at Butlin's, shift the idea of settlement towards modern holiday villages, with a significant presence of activities and services. However, the leap in scale detaches from the human community relationship one wanted to find in the first examples and certainly from the relationship with nature. Although the post-war period is seen as the golden age of the camps, it is not the most interesting for this research. On the other hand, the pioneering model maintains some elements that can still be updated: the dimensional relationship between the settlement system and the landscape, the desire to offer an "experiential" holiday and the "all-inclusive" offer, which other European experiences will then take up.

Free Time

Finally, the development of the theme of working holidays within the world of work should be considered. The first country to recognise paid holidays for workers was the United Kingdom. In 1871, the Bank Holiday Act added some days of paid holidays in addition to public holidays.

> It was thanks to the interest of Sir John Lubbock, banker and representative of the Liberal Party: the law defined the days shown in the table below as public holidays. Sir John was a keen cricketer and was a firm believer that bank employees should have the opportunity to attend and watch such matches: bank holidays included the dates when cricket matches were held in the villages of the region where Sir John grew up. The British population was so grateful to him that, for some time, he renamed the first bank holiday "S. Lubbock's Days".
>
> (Olmert, 1996, p. 170)[15]

The first state to devise a system of paid holidays valid for all workers was France, with a law written and promulgated in 1936. The agreements signed by Léon Blum and the French General Confederation of Production (CGPF) and the General Confederation of Labor (CGT) provided for the generalisation of collective agreements, the creation of staff representatives and a 12% increase in salaries and above all, the introduction of the 40-hour week and the granting of 15 days of paid leave. On June 6, 1936, Blum announced that he would file a paid vacation bill. Léo Lagrange, a socialist deputy from the north, Undersecretary of State for Leisure and Sport, dealt with the dossier. However, the Director of Labor at the Ministry of Labour, Charles Picquenard, wrote the text on the night of June 8. Introduced to the House and voted unanimously on June 11, it was adopted by the Senate eight days later by 295 votes to two. The law was promulgated on June 20 by Albert Lebrun, President of the Republic, and published in the *Official Gazette* on June 26. It provided that all employees who have worked continuously for one year in a factory were entitled to 15 days of paid leave per year.Those who had only been working for six months were entitled to one week. In addition, a daily allowance equal to the salary is foreseen. A circular dated July 6, 1936, specified that the ordinary holiday period is that of the school holidays (July 14–October 1), except for seasonal activities. Holidays formalise vacation time as a common right and consolidate the idea of travelling outside the city as a moment of relaxation. The holiday becomes another moment from everyday life within everyone's reach.

Also, given that train tickets were too expensive, Lagrange started negotiating with the train companies, creating a popular ticket with a 40% reduction. In 1936, 360,000 "Lagrange" tickets were issued for a total of 549,000 travellers. To facilitate stays by the sea and in the mountains, special trains were organised with a 60% reduction. A popular ticket was created with the 40-hour week and the birth of weekends.

Regarding accommodation, financial aid was provided to youth hostels; their number rose from 250 to 400 in one year. The number of overnight stays rose from 10,000 in 1935 to 26,000 in 1936. Winter sports were also democratised by Léo Lagrange (15,152 travellers to Mont-Dore instead of 4,535). Finally, note the development of the campsite. The emergence of free time for all was undoubtedly one of the greatest successes of the Popular Front[16].

In Italy, the topic was addressed for the first time in 1927 under the fascist regime with the Labor Charter. It was only with the 1948 Constitution that paid holidays were officially introduced as we understand them today[17]. The right to the "annual working period of paid rest" was ratified for the first time in Italy by the XVI provision contained in the Labor Charter, published in the *Official Gazette n°100* of April 30, 1927. Subsequently, the Italian Constitution established that every worker has a personal and inalienable right to a holiday period that he cannot renounce and must use (art. 36). The Constitution does not specify the minimum duration of this period (neither in the original text nor in subsequent additions). The primary law's reference on the subject was, for a long time, *article 2109* of the civil code ("rest period"), which reads:

1. The employee has the right to one day of rest each week, usually coinciding with Sunday.
2. He also has the right after one year of uninterrupted service to an annual period of paid leave, possibly continuous, for the time the employer establishes, considering the company's needs and the employee's interests. The duration of this period is established by law, corporate regulations and custom or according to equity.

A minimum of 28 days, implemented by all collective agreements, was introduced by Legislative Decree April 8, 2003 n. 66 and by the circular of the Ministry of Labor n.8 of 2005. Under article 10 of the legislative decree July 19 2004, n. 21, the employee has the right to paid holidays of at least four weeks, which cannot be liquidated economically. If the worker is not granted holidays, he has the right to be paid for the remaining days. In addition, the national collective bargaining agreements for the category can increase the annual holidays to which the worker is entitled.

Epilogue

The sum of these experiences results in the puzzle of a world in transition. This state of hybridisation, between the ordinary residential and the special one, between the natural and the artificial, remains a fundamental characteristic of open-air accommodation facilities and tourism in general. After the Second World War, the economic boom led, especially in Europe, to a significant development of tourist experiences related to the open air and campsite. In this period, the first large holiday companies and the first organised experiences of holiday villages developed. A list of pioneering examples from this point of view will now be illustrated, which deal with the theme of the holiday from an experiential and architectural point of view.

Below is the last protagonist of our three-way duel: the landscape. It will be presented as a list of well-known definitions of the landscape to avoid getting lost in random definitions, alongside some normative definitions, most of which are European. This final list is intended to give an idea of the importance of the landscape in the topic of tourism and open-air tourism in general.

ACT 2: PIONEERS OF OPEN-AIR HOSPITALITY

Open-air tourism involves dialogue between three entities:

- The tourist, who seeks an experience linked to the natural environment that generates a detachment from everyday life.
- The accommodation system, comprised of fixed (services) and mobile (residential units) parts, which must provide a temporary service.
- The landscape system, which acts as the primary visual and uses an attractor.

This complex relationship has developed inconsistently over the years on different fronts. On the one hand, some entrepreneurs have grasped the need to escape the world of work and capitalist society and have responded by proposing alternative holiday models. On the other hand, some projects have dealt with temporary accommodation systems, mainly linked to housing units grouped in small groups and reasoning with the landscape; in parallel, a specific sensitivity towards the landscape developed in Western society, codified in a normative way and some definitions. These experiences represent the starting cultural background for understanding the nature of these temporary cities.

The first historical experiences of the mass campsite are linked to the experience of holiday clubs and villages. The example of Club Med, among others, or Magic Villages, Club Mediterranee or Village Olympic are some of the most famous holiday villages organised with tents or small huts. In her book *The City Of Tourism*, Trillo illustrates the characteristics and history of some of these interventions excellently, such as the case of the Costa Smeralda and Club Med (Trillo, 2003). Furthermore, in the conference speech during ISUF 2022 "The city of entertainment as an experimentation field for improving the daily public space", (Capotorto and Trabattoni, 2022), the emphasis is placed on how some of these experiences are examples of an approach to open-air tourism, the most significant of these, that I would be remiss not to mention, are indeed that of *the Club Med* and *the Costa Smeralda.*

Club Med

Club Med is one of the most famous examples of open-air holidays. The experience of the Club Mediterranee, or Club Med, is related to those of the Magic Villages[18] and the Olympic Village[19]. The idea captured by the entrepreneurs was to allow Club members to find a place away from everyday life, both physically and mentally. All the strategies implemented in these examples aimed to counter a certain sense of loneliness and alienation generated by the capitalist industrial society. The "Club" was, above all, a form to give uniqueness to the group, with the choice to enhance shared moments such as meals and sleeping. The initial phases of these experiences were also linked to the choice of providing an economical service. In addition, the holiday wanted to be within everyone's reach, so the choice of using tents as accommodation was consistent.

The company created in 1950 by Gérard Blitz and Gilbert Triganò aimed to build a world away from everyday life. The "all-inclusive" formula implied the cancellation of everyday life and the construction of a housing "bubble" linked to holidays, entertainment and the landscape. The first village opened in Majorca was built with simple elements, tents and typical wooden tables. The idea of the Club (with an annual fee) was linked to the idea of a community to be built. In 1952, after the tents were set aside, thatched-roof Polynesian bungalows arrived. The architecture, which later became characteristic, referred to the idea of a tribe or a group. In 1955 the first Club outside the Mediterranean was inaugurated in Tahiti. In 1956, winter villages were introduced with the opening of the village of Leysin in Switzerland. In 1957 Gilbert Trigano inaugurated the village of Cefalù. Later, the Club expanded into the Caribbean and Canada.

Each resort offers a variety of services and activities within one package. This package includes accommodation, meals, use of the facilities and participation in sporting activities, games and shows. Club Med staff are referred to as GO (Gentils Organizer) in the resorts and are active day and night to entertain guests, called GM (Gentils Membres); these names help convey the feeling of belonging, even temporarily, to another reality.

This idea's incredible success inevitably led to a change in the philosophy of the service. Initially, exclusivity was linked to experience, anomalous or unusual, but economically it was within everyone's reach. In the second phase, the economic part is lost to support the costs associated with the incredible increase in members, and exclusivity also becomes linked to affordability. Its history after the 1970s can easily be found online[20]. The Club stopped being a Club in order to become a service agency.

The ability to grasp a still-existing need remains emblematic, even if expressed differently. The need to find a place different from

Figure 2.1 Costa Smeralda Landscape

everyday life means most European people have to find a place other than the urban one. Undoubtedly, one of the reasons for the success of open-air accommodation facilities, whether villages or campsites, is the definition of a protected context whose primary vocation is natural or linked to open space. For this reason, the definition of the identity of the open space is so vital for these structures. In this sense, it is interesting to review the experience of planning the Costa Smeralda in Sardinia, Italy, where an attempt was made to determine local identity by constructing "traditional" linguistic characters.

Costa Smeralda

The tourist phenomenon relating to the Costa Smeralda, a northeastern region of Sardinia, represents an emblematic case study concerning the construction of the landscape and architecture in favour of tourism promotion. In the history of Sardinia, the Costa Smeralda did not exist until 1962, the date of the official creation of the tourist resort. The Costa Smeralda is located in the historical region of Gallura, in the northeastern part of Sardinia, within the municipal limits of Arzachena, occupying 55km of coastline ranging from Cala Razza di Giuncu to Liscia di Vacca. The coast, that was sparsely inhabited for historical reasons,[21] was transformed into an exceptional tourist resort in the 1960s, aiming to attract another level of tourism. The strategy to achieve this result was building a non-existent architectural and natural vernacular landscape.

> As repeated several times, the paradox will be that those mentioned above "vernacular Esperanto" will be applied to a newly founded territory on the sparsely inhabited Gallura coast, going to look elsewhere for the elements of inspiration. Furthermore, they will pick up on the suggestions of neorealism when its prominent supporters (Quaroni, Ridolfi) will have abandoned it by now.
>
> (Cappai, 2014, p. 52)

The Costa Smeralda Consortium, founded in the 1960s, was born to guide the residential urban development of a specific geographical area, and, within a short time, they added to this aim that of safeguarding and increasing the value of that which was already existing.

> Although the pioneer of the Costa Smeralda is, Mr Duncan Miller, who is considered the official founder of the Costa and who will remain President of the Costa Smeralda Consortium for 30 years

> is Prince Karim Aga Khan, who at the time was twenty-six, had already been as successor Imam of the Ishmaelites, an important religious office for a faction of Muslims.
>
> (Cappai, 2014, p. 102)

These objectives have been pursued by controlling the environment from a landscape and building perspective by supplying a very high-level environmental and safety services system.

In 1969 the master plan of the Sardinian Consortium was made public, drawn up by the architect Luigi Vietti, in which an exciting question emerged regarding the aesthetic values underlying the management of the natural and built landscape. As a result, the regulation contains detailed guidelines for treating naturalness, employing lists showing the criteria for choosing tree essences based on a partition of urbanised areas and concerning creating new green areas.

> The firm purpose of conserving the natural vegetation of the places on the newly formed one and the intention of safeguarding the ecology and the natural aspect of the places with more incredible determination... these rules, while not prohibiting the introduction of different landscape elements... they set themselves the goal of avoiding too violent contrasts between the local landscape and the works due to human intervention[22].

The objective was to harmonise the natural vegetation already present with that belonging to the new interventions, thus avoiding environmental contrasts or imbalances. The study of the existing vegetation, accompanied by vegetation surveys, has allowed the development of protection methods.

The regulation was highly detailed, going so far as to indicate which plants were most important for the landscape (junipers, holm oaks, carob trees, etc.), where they had to be positioned and indicated with precision in the plans of the survey the state of affairs of the project. Another objective of the architectural commission was to define the character of the "Sardinian" landscape. The tree essences and their use and architectural characteristics were selected for this aim. These were chosen uncritically throughout the Sardinian territory (which has local differences) and generally tried to use an alleged "traditional Mediterranean style" including natural and artificial elements: "*it is recommended that the buildings be in harmony with the topography of the land and that excessively rigid forms that are difficult to integrate with the landscape of the coast are avoided*" (Trillo, 2003, p. 73). Therefore, the criterion to be applied is a balance between traditional architecture, orographic conditions and morphological conditions of the site. As Claudia Trillo writes,

> the natural product is a social product. The categories of wild and primitive become the matrix of a myth, which however is the result of a careful design work. The construction of the architectural space presents a similar conflict between the "natural" condition of the site and the new "built" configuration for the user, which manifests itself in the way of relating architecture for tourism to local architecture.
>
> (Trillo, 2003, p. 78)

As much as Prince Karim Aga Khan appreciated the work of Vietti and the other members of the committee, theirs remained a limited-scale vision, perhaps too subjective to flow into territorial planning in its entirety. The Prince entrusted Morgan Wheelock, the expert master planner in the landscape, and Hideo Sasaki, with signing the Costa Smeralda Master Plan project. The primary strategy of the Master Plan was, therefore, to concentrate any construction within the tourist clusters starting from the buildings that had already been built, to redesign a road infrastructure that connected these villages and followed the profile of the topography, and to limit the buildings in the spaces between the villages so that the infrastructure did not interfere with the only fundamental element of attraction of the place: the natural landscape (Cappai, 2014, p. 8).

Macro-themes will organise the Master Plan, understood as anthropic elements of intervention: the existing building, the road infrastructure and the open and leisure spaces. These deserve special attention in this discussion. Proper use of open space is the best guarantee against destructive actions or policies by adjacent landowners. In semi-wild areas, tourists do not have to recognise boundaries or property lines. Consideration should be given to extending a protection bond to open spaces with recreational use, including in areas beyond the legal boundaries of the CCS. In order to conserve the peculiarities of the area, some areas should be preserved by maintaining the natural contrast between the coastal areas and the mountains in order to reinforce the attractiveness of the resort through open spaces.

Recreational activity is considered key to the success of the resort (Cappai, 2014, p. 12).

The illustrated experiences show an approach to the theme of open-air accommodation that is linked to a need for abstraction from ordinariness through the definition of an identifiable context. The choices of Club Med portray the intention of another company, the possibility of being part of an exclusive group that belongs to an exclusive place and way of life. Costa Smeralda's urban planning and architectural design pursues the definition of a place by building an inexistent vernacular language. Through the definition of a "vernacular", the desire to define the identity of the place is pursued, and it is therefore vital both for the landscape and for nature.

The vernacular, as Rudofsky recalls, refers to a design without "architects", a primordial way of inhabiting the world. Inherent to the idea of vernacular is a particular contact with the earth and nature. There is a tendency, though, to combine this type of construction with an Arcadian vision of the relationship between man and nature, idealised as harmonious and serene. The enhancement of the place is sought, thus emphasising the importance of the natural context. Both proposed cases' objective is detachment from everyday life, obtained through social agreements and by constructing a univocal context.

Italian Touring Club (TCI)

Another interesting example to mention is the Italian Touring Club (TCI). Like its English and French namesakes, the Italian Club was also born as a cycling association. However, unlike the other two clubs (TCF and CTC), the Italian one, in addition to organising trips and activities for members, has been committed to the theme of accommodation, both temporary and otherwise.

The association was founded in 1894 in Milan under the name of Touring Club Ciclistico Italiano (TCCI) by a group of 57 cyclists, including Federico Johnson, who belonged to the Veloce Club Milano and who was the first director of the TCI[23]. The main aim of the TCI was the spread of the bicycle, seen as a new means of transport within everyone's reach, a symbol of modernity and an engine for the spread of tourism throughout the peninsula. Today, with around 280,000 members, it is one of Italy's tourist institutions with the most members. TCI also engages in improvement and concrete development of

Figure 2.2 Club Med Landscape

roads: cycle paths, installation of medical and first aid kits on main roads, and signage and embellishment of railway stations. With the beginning of the new century, the appearance of the automobile considerably widened their range of action: the TCI now also presents proposals for the establishment of National Parks, reforestation projects, solutions to new problems posed by the road network, and raises awareness against mass tourism in the country. Over time, the TCI has also increased its initiatives in order to regulate mass tourism flows that are directed almost exclusively to the largest and most overcrowded cities. As a result, touring guides, manuals and maps have become famous. 1914, for example, the Touring Map of Italy 1:250,000 was released, the first in Italy for exclusively touristic purposes.

The Italian Touring Club, then already in the first decades of its life, began to organise "social" holidays for its members, first with the historic "national excursions" that included stays in tented camps, then with real campsites in areas of great touristic-environmental value. These are temporary campsites, organised in tents for the duration of the holiday and therefore wholly removable. The first campsite organised by the TCI for its members was held in 1922 in Val Contrin, at the foot of the Marmolada: two weekly shifts saw 300 members take part. Since then, campsites organised by the TCI in the high mountains followed one another for 18 years, until 1939; these included destinations such as the Conca di By, in the Aosta Valley, at the foot of the Grand Combin (1923); the Fiorentina Valley, below Monte Pelmo (1925); the Sila Grande, within the sizeable state-owned forest of Fossiata (1928); on the occasion of the Sila Summer, Valsavarenche (1932); Val Martello (1934,); Val d'Ayas and Monte Rosa (1937); Tre Cime di Lavaredo (1938); and Gran Paradiso (1939)[24].

The interest in this collective system of use of the landscape is clear, and even if a technical description is missing, images of the campsites tell of small modern villages, similar to military camps. The entire settlement is designed as a service of necessity according to the use of the landscape. They are very basic stays at high altitudes (the one in Val Martello was located at 2264m, near the refuge that was then called Dux, today Nino Corsi), with large tents similar to those of the army that house many cots and a large tent/dining room with tables and benches for lunch reminiscent of military ones.

After the interlude of the War, the TCI restarted social holidays but focused its attention and efforts on seaside resorts. In 1947 it created a campsite organised in Marina di Campo on the island of Elba. This moved to Ischia (Na) and Fiascherino (Sp) two years later. In 1952, it returned by chance to the mountains, to Canazei, in Val di Fassa (Tn), but then resumed its marine vocation with the campsite in Marina di Ravenna from 1952 to 1956[25]. With the economic boom of the 1960s, members' expectations changed. Also, municipal regulations no longer allow the installation of authentic tent villages in intact places. By then the travelling campsite was becoming more and more challenging to implement and manage. The TCI then moved on to the creation of permanent campsites. The first was made in 1958 on the islands of Tremiti, in San Domino. The idea was to offer an environmentally friendly holiday where nature can be fully experienced. A village with tents and masonry structures for services was built on the 40,000m^2 site.

The Tremiti Islands were followed by the creation of two other villages, always in places of great naturalistic value; one on the island of La Maddalena, in Sardinia in 1967, of 62,000m^2, where a sector cannot be purchased but is obtained under a concession from Sardinia Region administration; and that of Marina di Camerota, in Cilento, between Capo Palinuro and Sapri, in 1968. The latter, purchased by Ermenegildo Zegna[26], is located in a 66,000m^2 centuries-old olive grove that slopes almost to the beach. Accommodations are primarily in tents in all three villages: these are lodge and Canadian-type tents with spartan cots inside. After that, the services are shared in some buildings built ad hoc.

In the mid-1960s, the TCI adopted a new arrangement: a particular tourist shed called a "shell" designed by the architect Roberto Menghi[27] in 1967, which would receive the Compasso D'oro award[28]. Shells invaded all three TCI villages, flanking rustic reed huts with thatched roofs, and presented themselves as a significant step forward in hospitality; they are available both in a single version and in one made up of two modules: "A real apartment, two L-shaped beds, a small table, two sets of shelves at the foot of the beds. Three windows, two slits at the bottom and a vent at the top, to facilitate ventilation"[29]. The three villages host up to 300 people. The shared activities are all linked to nature, and the moments of community are delegated to those in need, services and food.

The TCI experience, even for members only[30], is essential in the Italian panorama to understand the relaunch of a holiday "in nature" but full of comforts and services. The TCI's activities, even if aimed at satisfying the members, were often aimed at preserving the natural context because the value of that context was also recognised from an experiential point of view of the holiday.

Figure 2.3 Touring Club Landscape

ACT 3: PIONEERS OF ARCHITECTURAL SOLUTIONS

The architectural decline linked to mass tourism experienced its critical debate, especially in Italy, in the 1960s, when tourism began to impact the territory. In the article *Homo Abitus Naturae*, Ernesto Nathan Rogers, in opening an intellectual debate on the conservation of the territory, cites some data concerning the number of tourists:

> The presence of Italian and foreign tourists between the years 1952 and 1963 increased from 34 to 76.3 million, writes Rogers, statistics warn fearfully, because, even if they were a little exaggerated, they always represent a trend index: in 1963 there were 922,000-bed places, in 1968, in five years, 1260,000 will be needed.
>
> (Rogers, 1964, p. 807)

The fear induced by these numbers leads architects to a qualitative reflection on land consumption. Again using Rogers' words, "It is therefore a matter of inventing a new landscape for the 50 million Italians who now live there" (Rogers, 1964, p. 804). The dilemma is about something other than building or not, but how to do it and respond to an obvious request. Underlying this is the awareness and faith that design and planning skills allow for maintaining that balance between the built and the natural element which defines the Italian landscape, according to Rogers. "If there is a country partly empowered by man (homo hadditus naturae), this is Italy…" (Rogers, 1964). From a design point of view, the debate is divided between a rationalist approach and one defined as neorealist.

This debate, started in the sixties, includes some reflections on architectural language and settlement planning, extends from newly-founded neighbourhoods to tourist villages, tourist enclaves, and is still actual today. The beginning of that phenomenon gave life to what is possible to define as an "intermittent city", one that is super crowded in the high season and uninhabited for the rest of the year.

Some examples of these achievements (such as the projects of the Valtur villages of Ostuni (1967–1969) and Isola Capo Rizzuto (1967–1969) by the architect Luisa Anversa; the project by the BBPR studio (Belgiojoso, Banfi, Peressutti and Rogers) for the tourist development plan of Capo Stella, on the Island of Elba; the "Il Gualdo" subdivision plan (1961–1963) by Ludovico Quaroni; the "Poggio le Mandrie" subdivision plan (1961–1963) by Ludovico Quaroni) are paradigmatic of a settlement approach that can still be updated.

The dialectic of any critics will be contingent on a comparison of style between the neorealism[31] of Ridolfi and Quaroni and a greater rationalism that can be seen in the projects of the architect Luisa Anversa and Lucio Barbera. For example, one can compare the Martella di Quaroni village projects and the Valtur villages in Ostuni or Capo Rizzuti[32] by Anversa and Barbera. Quaroni's architectural research is based on the vernacular characteristics of the village and the hamlet (in the forms and materials, but also the spatial visions). The recovery of an idea of the vernacular in a sort of emphasis is a trait that will often be found in tourist architecture. The idea of an ideal Arcadian vernacular architecture that qualifies the veracity of the place, and therefore of the experience, is at the basis of many of the Club Med tourist villages, for example. On the other hand, the architects Anversa and Barbera seek a rationalist approach in their creations, both in formal definition and settlement. The in-line or courtyard approach is developed as a recognisable settlement matrix and restarts from the local typology to generate the modern context.

In Ostuni, in particular, it is an existing farmhouse that defines the courtyard settlement system that defines the spatiality of the village. The search for the spatial dimension of the village is also the basis of the development plan of Gualdo by Ludovico Quaroni. Beyond the political events concerning this project, the capillary system proposed by Quaroni, organised on a square grid in a pedestrianised and low-density context, is emblematic of an approach to building that seeks a relationship with the compensating void. The idea of the village and the hamlet that underlies many vernacularisms, such as the works of Luigi Vietti, is reinterpreted here rationally.

Campsites remain unrelated to this debate. In general, due to their nature of being linked to the void, open-air accommodation facilities are rarely, in Italy, are they the object of planning.

Some virtuous projects have been selected to define this type of holiday's historical and cultural background, which is intrinsically linked to the natural landscape. The proposed projects are significant either for the theme treated, similar if not coinciding with that of open-air accommodation facilities, or because they, in any case, exemplify a settlement system that is linked to the landscape and the temporality of living. The cases that will be presented translate the topic of open-air holidays, both when focused on the housing object and when developed on the entire structure, in order to try to modernise the design approach. The proposed projects will be discussed, thus emphasising more than the historical event that concerns them in the strategies related to the settlement system, the architectural language and the relationship with the landscape. Although they do not have similar dimensions, they are comparable if evaluated according to these constants. The common trait is the author's design. In some way, the aim is to define a theoretical basis by acknowledging how recognised architects have dealt with the theme. For this reason, the chronological period of reference starts from the 1930s and almost reaches the present day, with the project by Luigi Snozzi for the tourist village in Sardinia. The scales of the projects are also different, ranging from the minimal sector of Le Corbusier to the almost urban settlement of the GATPAC.

Attention must be placed on the relationship between time and living with the aim of the enhancement of nature. This trinomial involves housing solutions that are sometimes minimal and linguistic research that tends towards the vernacular. However, it also involves the priority definition of the relationship with the landscape, a relationship possible thanks to the reduced time of living on vacation.

Within the examples' description, it's possible to list some fundamental keywords in relation to the potential improvement of outdoor tourism:

- Relation with landscape;
- Planning;
- Architectural language;
- Perspective;
- Enclosure

City of Repos y Vacances – 1934/1936 – GATPAC

Keywords: planning, architectural language

The Ciutat de Repos y Vacances (the City of Rest and Holiday) is an urban project promoted by the GATCPAC (Group of Catalan Architects and Technicians for the Progress of Contemporary Architecture). The project involved the construction of a real city south of Barcelona, conceived as a holiday resort for both long and short periods. The project had been located on the beaches of the municipalities of Castelldefels, Viladecans and Gavà (Baix Llobregat), near Barcelona, which it would have been connected to thanks to an extension of the Gran Via.

The project starts from an urban scale of sectionalisation and organisation of the territory, but reaches an architectural scale, proposing architectural solutions for all types of buildings. The long stretch of the coast is organised into zones. The main road that arrives from Barcelona crosses the main artery that runs parallel to the coast at a distance of 1500m from the sea. Developing the new urban sector in this land space will be proposed. Following an orthogonal layout, the GATPAC defines four main zones with different functional organisations: Zona de Cura and Repos; Banys area; Zone of the week cap; and Zona de residencia. First of all, the treatment area is located in the far west, somewhat isolated from the rest of the city, and was intended as a health and rest area, with various facilities for patient care, such as sanatoriums, clinics and health centre pavilions. The seaside area is located in the city centre and was conceived as where people would go to spend a day at the beach. It is here where the bus station, the railway station and the administration building of the city are located. We also find all kinds of sports and leisure facilities, such as football and tennis fields, a stadium, swimming pools or the open-air cinema. Thirdly, the weekend area is designed for short stays. There are hotels and several sports and leisure facilities, such as more football pitches, a running track and another open-air cinema. Finally, the residential area was made up of apartments or single-family houses, as it was intended for more extended stays. As for services, we find swimming pools and a golf course. The GATPAC proposes to wholly maintain the existing pine forest on the coast and to implement a number of trees.

One of the characteristic elements of the project, which stands out in the weekend area, is that of the demountable or removable house. It was a modular product, which we can consider as industrial, as it can be manufactured on a large scale and in series. The goal was to use minimal living space to reduce production costs while maintaining dignity. The GATPAC does not define where to put these housing typologies; they only identify the macro-area. However, the purpose of these objects is to allow the inhabitants to rediscover contact with nature in the simplicity of living.

The GATPAC aims to create a place detached from everyday life, a place of rest linked to nature, easily accessible and within everyone's reach.

Hotel San Michele – 1938 – Gio Ponti, Bernard Rudofsky

Keywords: architectural language; relation with landscape

In 1938, Gio Ponti and Bernard Rudofsky finalised the Hotel San Michele project, a "hotel in the woods" to be built on the slopes of Monte Solaro, between Capri and Anacapri. The work is part of the architectural research that unites the two architects and is linked to the idea of the Mediterranean house. Rudofsky's studies and Ponti's proposals for the ideal home and the beach house that led to the construction of the house in Positano and the house in Procida can be found in the project for the Hotel San Michel.

The proposal, never built but published the following year in the *Architecture* magazine, envisages the construction of a central nucleus that houses the collective services and a series of small independent units arranged in the wooded area of the island, 300m above sea level, overlooking the Gulf of Naples. Each unit, connected to the core of services thanks to a network of paths through the vegetation, establishes a unique relationship with the context in which it is located, generating a variation on the theme to adapt to the site and nature. The idea was that of a deconstructed hotel, where the rooms become mini-lodgings developed in the woods, and the corridors run in the open air. It followed the then-current theme of the widespread hotel and what would later be developed in the holiday villages. Moreover, more than anything else, the theme of integration in the natural contrast enhances the landscape.

> Italian Nature – says Ponti – is sacred, and to respect it, it is necessary to understand it in all its components; only then will we be able to build an architecture that belongs to it; only then will we be able to build 'walls which, by the sea, will be sisters of pines, palms, agaves, olive trees and at the same time they will be an abstract play of the imagination.
>
> (Mucelli, 2017)

The search for an expression, which could give a "Caprese" alternative to the style of a seaside holiday through its design choices, is reflected in a vision that places the relationship between architecture and landscape at the centre of the proposal.

The central nucleus of the hotel is a courtyard building. The premise of open space included in the architecture, protected from heat and wind, becomes the recurring theme, applied to different scales, even in small apartments designed as hospitality spaces. In the collective building, it is a square; it is a meeting and gathering place. In individual houses, it is a private courtyard. These atypical rooms, or small bungalows, develop tortuously in the ground, respecting the contour lines but presenting as real tiny houses—built-in masonry with small windows. The domestic open space mediates the panoramic view of the place. Around the central void of the "square", a collective place par excellence, the drawings represent a series of services, a bar, a restaurant with a terrace, common rooms for hotel guests and the home of the manager, whom Ponti defines as the "resident" and who identifies with the figure of a gentleman who takes care of his guests (Mucelli, 2017). The construction system and finishes recall Mediterranean architecture; the white wall that protects the courtyard of the housing units is the mediation tool with nature, which maintains the role of architecture and finds a balance with the natural context and the Landscape.

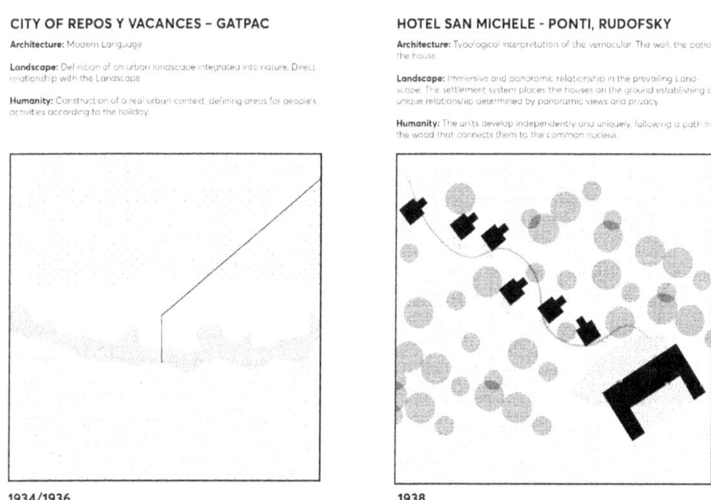

Figure 2.4 Pioneers of Architecture Diagram 1

Desert Hill Motel – 1947 – Albert Frey

Keywords: perspective; relation with landscape; architectural language

Finding information about Albert Frey's Desert Hill motel takes a lot of work. The job was given to him by Raymond Cree, a school superintendent turned real estate developer in the Palm Springs area, who bought 12 acres of land outside Palm Springs in 1947. He commissioned Frey to build a desert resort in Palm Springs, which was then the subject of a lot of attention, especially from wealthy Los Angeles residents. The resort was to include a main building and a series of smaller bungalows. Frey, born in Switzerland and moving to Palm Springs in the early 1930s, had already established himself as one of the best modern architects in the area. Throughout his career, he designed several notable buildings in Palm Springs, including the Raymond Loewy House, the Hidden Frey and his home, the Frey House II. The development of that style that defined Desert Modernism was the synthesis of Frey's "modern" training (he had worked in Le Corbusier's studio) and particular attention to the climate and landscape of Palm Springs. The project was never implemented.

In 1955, a year after his wife's death, Cree, aged 82, asked Frey to revisit the hotel property, this time to design his residence. The Cree House is a clear example of Albert Frey's modern style. However, if understood as part of a vision linked to the landscape intended as a sensory function, it represents an interesting example of a relationship with the landscape.

Clear three-dimensional visualisation of the Desert Hill resort remains in the Cree House. However, it is possible to read this in not only the layout but also the architectural intentions. The modern language of pilots and simple shapes hybridises with Frey's training, the introduction of light and innovative materials (aluminium). The plan develops on a slope. A main enclosure is defined at street level, with an entrance gate and ample parking space. The main building detaches from this first entrance level, leaning on a rocky promontory and creating a collective area with the tennis court (services). It is safe to assume that the bungalows assumed to be resort accommodations are built like the Cree house (like Frey's other buildings). The style system, the light materials and the use of colour integrating into the context are some architectural strategies linked to constructive and compositional choices. This approach is economical as there is no need to create a flat building platform, which requires costly excavation and retaining walls. Instead, the houses touch the ground with only part of the floor and develop a large outdoor terrace.

The prospective relationship with the landscape is evident and unambiguous. Taking the Cree House as an example again, the bungalows overlook the "predominant landscape", in this case, the Palm Spring valley, and the road is led sinuously, accompanying the slope, to all the houses. In the context of Palm Springs in the 1930s–1950s, the use of the car and the possibility of having the car next to the house was fundamental. As will happen with all the houses in the Case Studio House, the theme of the parking space becomes an integrated architectural solution. In the Cree House, the large terrace that leads the domestic space towards the landscape also protects the car.

On the opposite side, another external space is more intimate and private. As in the Cree House, the external space of the house is equivalent in size to the internal one and is the tool through which a dialogue is opened with the landscape.

Unitès de Camping – 1949 – Le Corbusier

Keywords: architectural language

Le Corbusier's project for a "unitè de Camping" is minimal, and to be read, as with the Unitè d'Habitation in Marseille, as a manifesto project. The problem that the architect wants to answer is that of using otherwise unusable land for tourism and, therefore, panoramic purposes, whilst also being in close proximity to the sea. Le Corbusier had already conducted this research with the projects for the ROQ and ROB summer houses in Cap Saint-Martin. With the ROQ and ROB work, the Swiss architect proposed working where the land was not accessible or usable, developing houses on stilts, thus avoiding further compromising the land of the Côte d'Azur, which was already "devastated" by houses and villas.

The houses, long and narrow in shape, could be developed alone or in series and adapt to the sloping terrain favouring the sea view. The construction patent, called 226x226x226, which was born using the measurements of the Modulor and defines a modular metal structure system, guaranteed the development on several levels freeing up the interiors to optimise the contribution of sunlight.

The campsite unit instead develops the theme of minimum receptive space. It is a system of five rooms for two people with an internal sink, built on stilts and merged to define a single block. The building consists of a wooden structure that houses the five units, placed on reinforced concrete stilts straddling the rectangles, with dry embankment walls characteristic of the region. The internal space is minimal and organised with fixed furnishings, as Le Corbusier would later do for his Cabanon, the study he created for himself by recovering a wooden warehouse. The spatial idea is linked to the constrained visibility of the landscape. As with the Cabanon, the campsite units are not equipped with large openings, but small windows that frame the landscape as in a pictorial frame. The sink placed in the middle defines the fulcrum of the 8m^2 space, designed for two people and two beds.

The idea that one reads when looking at the project is one of infrastructure for a holiday, a bit like the cabins of the sea, a housing system reduced to less than the minimum. After the architect's death, the clients added five small kitchens under the houses to make the Unitè more independent and similar to a beach house. The wooden building with an isolated sheet metal roof relates to the landscape in a panoramic way without seeking mediation. The chromatic choices of Le Corbusier, combined with the formal volumetric language, the definition of the openings and the finishes, make the architecture of the "Unitè de Camping" solid and recognisable in the Landscape. However, the space is all facing the sea, having a single windowed front opposite the entrance.

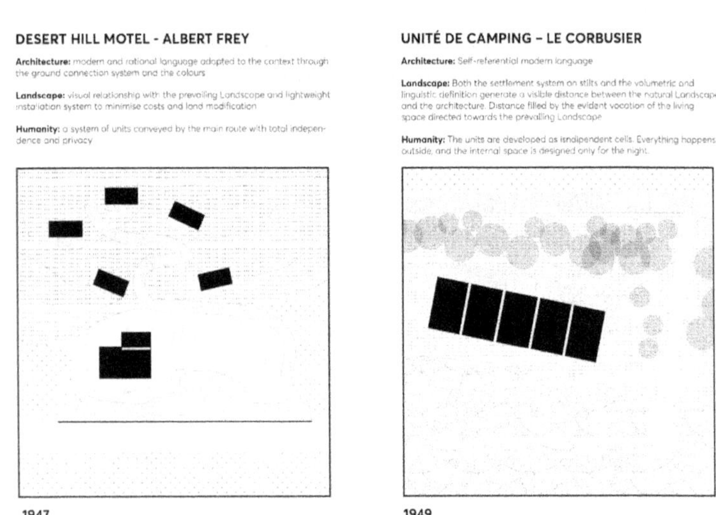

Figure 2.5 Pioneers of Architecture Diagram 2

Eni Village Borca di Cadore – 1954 – Edoado Gellner, Carlo Scarpa

Keywords: relation with landscape; architectural language

The Eni Village of Borca di Cadore represents a virtuous example of an open-air accommodation system in a context of great landscape value, which focuses on a solid relationship with the surrounding nature. More than a real accommodation facility, it should be considered a workers' village, resulting from a visionary, strategic ambition proposed by Enrico Mattei in collaboration with the architect Edoardo Gellner and Carlo Scarpa between the 1950s and 1960s.

The Eni complex occupies more than 100,000m^2 of woods at the foot of Monte Antelao and is equipped with different structures. The organic-social criterion adopted by Mattei was transferred to the project by Gellner, who completely redefined it, at every level, from the urban organisation to the architectural one. The main structures of the site are the Colony (30,000m^2), the Church of Nostra Signora del Cadore (designed together with Scarpa), the hotel, the campsite with fixed tents, 280 single-family houses and the residence. The complex designed by Gellner also envisaged the construction of a further 330 villas and a social centre, which were never built due to the slowdown in construction following Mattei's death in 1962. Instead, the single-family villas built were all constructed between 1955 and 1963. They are of different sizes and types to accommodate more or less numerous families. They are divided into four groups in order to create neighbourhood and socialising areas while guaranteeing privacy. They all have a mainly horizontal development to better integrate into the landscape. Transverse walls in concrete characterise the prevailing structural typology; the roof has a single, slightly sloping pitch, while the elevations have large windows opening onto a loggia on the façade so that the interior spaces are very bright and placed in relation to the surrounding landscape.

Finally, the campsite is located in the highest part of the area, at an altitude of about 1,200m. It comprises four "fixed tents" groups, each accommodating up to six beds. The huts have an isosceles triangular section. The layers that cover them are made with wooden planks. The planimetric scheme is quincunx to allow each module to distance itself as much as possible from the closest one and overlook a small strip of the mountain landscape. These small bungalows develop under the trees, following the lay of the land. The integration with the natural context is total so as to modify the architecture, which translates the elements of Alpine architecture into a modern key. The gabled roof thus becomes the complete form of the bungalow. These houses are positioned on stone walls to avoid damaging the ground by applying an extremely modern strategy: nature, which represents the prevailing landscape, remains as uncontaminated as possible.

Campsite Fusina – 1957 – Carlo Scarpa

Keywords: planning, architectural language

The campsite project was entrusted to Carlo Scarpa in 1957 and is one of the Venetian architect's lesser-known creations. The functional program envisaged the construction of the circular-plan tourist reception, the bar-restaurant and a service block that includes a washing area, seven service units and three pentagonal showers. The campground has been around since 1960 and is still in operation. It is not easy in a Scarpa project to proceed without describing the architectural details, which are always admirable. However, from a settlement point of view, this intervention is nonetheless very interesting if it is seen as a territorial sign concerning the use of the territory.

The Fusina campsite is situated over a peninsula at the end of the Naviglio del Brenta. The land on which the campsite develops is therefore closed on three sides by water, two of which are for industrial and transport use; that of the Naviglio and that of the ferry boat terminal. Beyond the architectural choices, the shoe work defines the boundary of the campsite, using the architecture to identify the entrance axis, which also marks the extreme edge of the accommodation area. The axis of the services, of the reception of the whole shoe intervention, closes the virtual square defined by the peninsula, marking the limit from which to develop the accommodation areas of the units. The building is intended to welcome visitors and has a circular plan which determines the starting point of the central organisational axis. The bar-restaurant building is the second architectural episode and stands on the left of the tree-lined avenue developing parallel to it. It has an articulated system with partition walls in plastered blocks and exposed brick intersected by horizontal planes at different levels. The middle part of the building looks towards the lagoon, following the direction of a second avenue defined by regular hedges perpendicular to the main one. The service block is divided into a sequence of volumes and open spaces, which include, starting from the south-west, an area of washrooms crowning the central room intended for the infirmary, a series of seven modular units containing pairs of bathrooms separated by a shower compartment with a pentagonal plan obtained by smoothing a square placed diagonally to the main front and, finally, a space with three outdoor showers, as many foot washers and some urinals. The washroom area has a rectangular courtyard with a long side parallel to the main avenue. At the centre of the courtyard stands the volume of the infirmary, made up of two independent bodies connected by a transversal portico.

There is a clear relationship with the landscape; since the establishment of the services, faced with the situation of the tents and, in general, temporary habitations such as caravans and trailers, remained the ordering element of the campsite. From this clean and precise line, it was possible to develop an organic landscape that did not fear the immanent chaos of the self-management of tourists. However, the inclusion of mobile homes in this ecosystem highlights the intrinsic problem of this housing system. The houses, even if temporary and removable, determine a clear relationship with the landscape, which conditions the context for at least 7–8 years (the life of the industrial

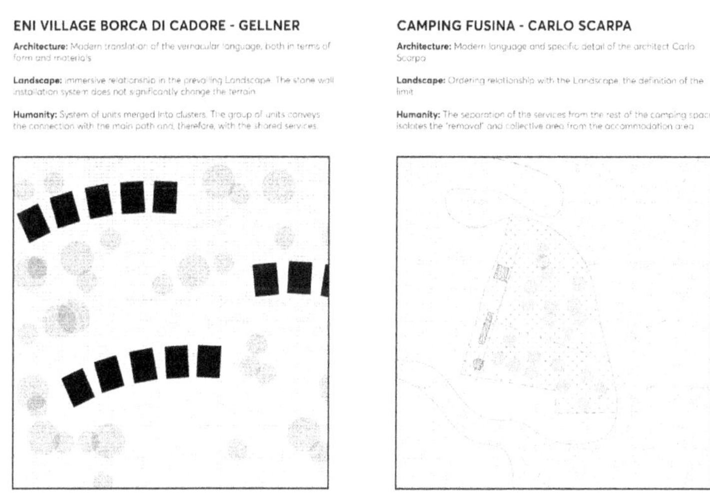

Figure 2.6 Pioneers of Architecture Diagram 3

product). In the Fusina campsite, the houses are positioned in independent clusters, losing the relationship with the open space and even more with the initial settlement system underlying the architectural intervention.

Capsule Village Resort in Usami – 1972 – Kiro Kurokawa

Keywords: perspective; relation with landscape; architectural language

The Metabolist[33] approach to the idea and design of the city is based on the theme of soil replication, a different and artificial ground. This ideological choice, which responds to specific socio-political and geographical conditions of post-World War II Japan (Koolhaas and Olbricht, 2022), today ideally marries well with a sustainability strategy of the non-consumption of land. Japan's massive post-War reconstruction efforts and government support for industrial development certainly played a significant role in establishing these models for building adaptable and reconfigurable architectures based on straightforward, mass-produced capsules. Most characteristically described for the Nagakin Capsule Tower (1970), but also explored for the Capsule Village (1972) and the Concrete Capsule House (1975), the capsules were designed as complete technological habitable containers to be inserted into an infrastructure or shared megastructure. In addition, each megastructure was designed as a foundation and conduit for the implantation or detachment of prefabricated boxes as the city grew or needs evolved. The Capsule Village, designed to accommodate leisure homes in a plug-and-play pod format, represents this metabolite approach to the soil in a very emblematic way. Specifically linked to the context and function, the project, that could appear futuristic, touches on highly topical issues.

It is, in fact, in its integration with the landscape that the Leisure Resort Village of Kurokawa should be interpreted as an integration without contact, but balanced on disinterested co-presence. A large-scale three-dimensional truss spanned intermediately placed concrete supports, tracing a steep topography that outlines a field of potential housing outlets. The megastructure touches the ground sporadically, following the slope and leaving room for the trees to grow. The access road connects the suspended cluster system. The clusters develop, favouring isolation and independence, ensuring that the housing units do not dialogue with each other but instead with the landscape overview.

Each capsule consists of a monocoque measuring 3m x 6m and is organised according to three housing functions: hygiene, nutrition and sleep. The mechanical box-like aesthetic exemplifies the designer's fascination with space-age imagery. Present in the Capsule Tower and Capsule Village, the simple rectangular geometry associated with the dwelling reduced the house to a no-frills functional unit, a type of micro-architecture that integrated home and furniture into an ergonomic whole.

The Capsule Village develops along the mountain. A single access route becomes the system of collective spaces, presumably linked to a large panoramic terrace. The clusters of 6 houses develop in parallel following the slope. To cover the height difference, the technical infrastructure that supports the capsules is also a pedestrian road infrastructure. Vehicle mobility is conveyed with a single access point while all the houses, which do not have private outdoor space but are summarised in the capsule, are accessible only for pedestrians.

Coastal Tourist Village – 2002 – Luigi Snozzi

Keywords: relation with landscape; enclosure; architectural language

The project for a coastal tourist village by Luigi Snozzi is part of design research to enhance the territory by rethinking the elements that define that same territory. After dealing with fascist foundation cities such as Carbonia, both didactically using them as a place of study for students, and professionally, through the construction of the interchange pole, Luigi Snozzi confronted himself with the landscape of the Sinis in the Oriastense area. The landscape is recognised for its large scale primary elements, thus relating the architectural scale to that of the landscape. As Luigi Snozzi explains,

> as often happens to me on my first visit to the place, I asked myself just one question: how come I realise I'm in Sardinian territory? We found four elements on the spot that speaks of Sardinia: the nuraghes, the novenari, the Romanesque churches and the watchtowers. All these elements have something in common: they are pure geometric shapes, they are made of stone and are scattered throughout the territory.
>
> (Fonti and Mameli, 2012, p. 42)

The project to define a typological intervention was born from this reading of the territory, of a receptive structure that is constantly repeated along the Sardinian coasts. Again following the words of Snozzi:

> We have thought of creating new villages, which have the same characteristics found in the other elements of the territory: pure architectural forms, building materials, stone ... and diffusion in the territory ... each village enclosed by cyclopean walls ... from the sea, it appears with its long wall highlighting the lay of the land.
>
> (Fonti and Mameli, 2012, p. 43)

Like all of Snozzi's architecture, the tourist village in Sardinia also wants to be radical and critical. The relationship with the landscape is evident. The boundary wall that develops along the coast appears as a sign that identifies man's presence, but without proceeding in the search for a fake vernacular, as has already been shown in Costa Smeralda. From the wall rises a white tower which, taking up that punctual relationship of visual measurement of the territory, like the watchtowers already do, defines a scale relationship between

CAPSULE VILLAGE IN USAMI - KUROKAWA

Architecture: Modern language with the metabolism approach to the Capsule

Landscape: Separation from the Landscape. The settlement does not touch the ground; follow the morphology to get the best view.

Humanity: The organisation of isolated Capsule aims to guarantee the whole privacy and isolation even in the proximity of the living units

1972

COASTAL TOURIST VILLAGE - SNOZZI

Architecture: Self-referential modern language inspired by local architecture

Landscape: Relationship of detachment and dialogue. The intervention has a recognisable identity that fits with the scale of the prevailing Landscape.

Humanity: Human space is a landscape in its own right, enclosed, protected within high walls, defining an oasis, separated from the outside.

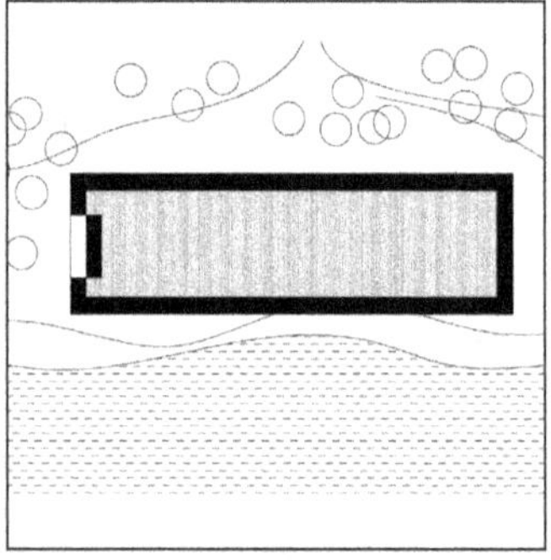

2002

Figure 2.7 Pioneers of Architecture Diagram 4

architecture and landscape. The village is an introverted landscape in its own right and independent. It dialogues culturally with the area's history, takes up human rather than natural references, imposing itself with the certainty of a balance guaranteed by a dimensional scale factor.

The total synthesis of Snozzi's project, which may appear excessive when compared with a conservative landscape sensitivity, must, however, be evaluated alongside that occupation of the territory with myriads of small units, which in any case occupy the territory. For Snozzi, there is no need to hide in the landscape when you can establish a balanced relationship.

ACT 4: LANDSCAPE'S LAWS AND ORDER

From a figurative aesthetic point of view, it is possible to say that the concept of landscape took shape in the 18th century in France. Marc Desportes explains that it relates to the possibility of visiting nature away from the city. The development of a study that deals with roads (*Bureau des ponts et chaussees*[34]) no longer only as a communication system but also as a travel system changes the way nature becomes landscape. "At the beginning of the century, the Landscape designated a type of painting and not a site" (Desportes, 2008, p. 50).

"Landscape" ceases to be a pictorial representation and is definitively linked to the perception of the natural element. In this sense, the "*Strada dei Lumi*" (Desportes, 2008, p. 78) functions as a tool to reveal, a perspective apparatus such as those used in the art of gardens. The road establishes an active synergy between the spectator and the show. "The meaning of the road is built when the traveller catches the elements that have attracted his attention" (Desportes, 2008, p. 71). The relationship between landscape and travel is expressed in this synergy. Expectations determine a relationship. If the painting anticipated and then described the expectations of the traveller of the late 18th century who began a journey outside the city, today, the landscape has taken the form of a syllogistic symbolism. All that is natural is landscape and beyond. In scientific descriptions, landscape is understood as a set of natural and anthropic elements. Everything is landscape, perhaps precisely because, as Lucius Burckhardt says, the landscape is in the eye of the beholder. The satisfaction of expectations determines the recognition and elevation of the natural landscape.

"There is an unpainted landscape in our heads, the fruit of education and reading, which allows us to perceive the surrounding environment as a landscape and impart meaning to it" (Burkhardt, 2019, p. 159). The theme of landscape has become more complex over the years. From an aesthetic approach to nature, as in classical gardens, it has been enriched with contents and ethics. The aesthetic approach of the vegetable element, which above all involves architecture, is confronted with a more botanical theory. Patrick Blanc's green walls coordinate plant essences to build a chromatic landscape, which supports the architecture in constructing the urban landscape. Patrick Blanc is considered by all to be a great artist, a designer and the inventor of the modern green wall. His works are botanical experiments using plant material as a composition tool.

On the other hand, Gilles Clement's theories propose a spontaneous landscape focused on the potential of pre-existing essences. The idea of a "*garden in movement*" (Clement, 2011) is endowed with autonomous rules and manifestations in which continuous changes and evolutions occur through the activity of the gardener who guides its structure. For Clement, the idea of human work is not in contrast to the essences considered invasive, but in coherence with them, assuming their prevaricating existence. Likewise, according to Clément, the "*planetary garden*" (Clement, 2008) represents a new paradigm in which the relationships between the garden, the landscape and nature are articulated according to a new configuration. The Third Landscape fits this vision of landscape as a residual space in which plants and animals that find no refuge elsewhere are welcomed (Clement, 2004). The garden is the metaphor for an autonomous landscape that asserts itself thanks to the intrinsic force of nature, which man can direct.

Following Clement's line, Piet Oudolf's projects define controlled contexts built with the image of the wild landscape. Piet Oudolf practices a naturalistic approach to gardening, placing the aesthetic-attractive impact and the seasonal duration of the plant at the centre of his research (Oudolf and Kingsbury, 2013). His activity is mainly based on the combination of perennial plants, i.e. those that do not have a short life cycle but last all year round.

The general idea of the landscape is therefore confronted with a cultural aspect, determined both by the expectations of those who look at and read the landscape, and by the whole literary and media substratum. However, it is also confronted with a botanical and ecological approach to the natural element, which also finds expression in a regulatory and theoretical approach. Maintaining the natural habitat requires, when implementing regulations of parks and protected areas, the conservation intervention of the existing essences, even in an additional phase. This is not a reinvention of the landscape, but a reorganisation of it using the given elements.

In the tourism sector, the expectation of the landscape is a crucial factor in the storytelling of the holiday. The term "landscape" is associated with "natural", even if superficially and sometimes improperly. In fact, with "natural", we often tend to associate a spontaneous plant system or, in any case, one antithetical to the anthropic one. This superficial vision generates misunderstandings. The Italian landscape, for example, and much of the European one, is, as we know, a mixture of man-made and nature. Some now-iconic landscapes are, in fact, the work of man. Think, for example, of the Italian pine forests. This tree system is recognised and "sold" worldwide as a system peculiar to some Italian areas, such as the Adriatic or Tuscan coast. The pine forests are a protected landscape, understood as a natural element of the value and identity of the territory. With pine forests, we refer to an arboreal context consisting of maritime pines that are found along the coast. Although some examples of spontaneous pine forests exist, most Italian pine forests result from a human activity. The Tuscany case, and that of Ravenna, are two very clear examples[35].

In Roman times, pine forests were exploited in order to produce timber to be used in arsenals and building activity. Antonio Gabrielli (1993) identifies in the Dogana dei Paschi di Siena statute the oldest evidence of pine forests in Tuscany, found in the stretch of the coast between Pian d'Alma and Orbetello:

> In the mid-17th and 19th centuries, the spread of pine forests followed the rhythm of the hydraulic reclamation of the coastal plains. Once the drainage works were completed, the pine trees were sown along the coastal dunes so that the pine forest would consolidate them and simultaneously constitute a protective band from the sea winds for the agricultural crops behind them. Up until the early years of the last century, there was an increase in the areas of coastal pine forests due both to additional plantings on dunes, but also to the expansion of these forest crops to the detriment of lowland deciduous forests that were located in the adjacent areas[36].

As a result of the many plantations made between the end of the 19th century and the beginning of the 1900s, the collection and trade of pine nuts in Tuscany were flourishing, reaching considerable commercial levels even worldwide: the pine forests were at that time 40–80 years old, and therefore production was at a maximum. After 1950, the Tuscan coastal pine forests were mainly attributed a landscape value, attempting to reconcile the new touristic enhancement with naturalistic conservation. A system built and constituted by man today is identified as a typical landscape. The pine forest of Follonica or Roccamare is praised as an example of uncontaminated nature.

> The exclusivity of this place has kept the pine forest intact, as well as the coast in front: the beach has remained "austere", walking on

> the shoreline, you notice many half-ruined wooden huts, where the guests of the houses that go down to the sea seek shelter from the sun, sitting on minimal benches. All very spartan and wild[37].

The same goes for the Ravenna pine forest established by monks between the 10th and 14th centuries to compensate for the maritime dunes formed with alluvial materials. Four extensive pine forests were formed, each entrusted to the care of a monastery or abbey: the pine forests of San Vitale, San Giovanni, Classe and Cervia. Their surface increased from 1,800 hectares to 7,000, for over 30km and a depth of a few kilometres. In his treatise on pine forests (*Civil history of the Ravenna pine forests 1774*), Francesco Ginanni[38] illustrates that the four pine forests extended over about 7,400 hectares without interruption from the bed of the river Lamone to the north up to Cervia. Over the years, for technical reasons (the need for fuel) and for military reasons, the surface of the pine forests was more than halved.

In the 1900s, the government reclaimed the land in the pine forest, recognising its historical and artistic value and proceeding with reforestation of the damaged areas. After the First World War, the pine forest took on its current appearance: a wood that unfolds along the coast. After the Second World War, the wooded area, due to human intervention, was divided into several pine forests, not contiguous to each other. The two historic pine forests included in the municipality of Ravenna, that of San Vitale and of Classe, occupy an area of approximately 2,000 hectares; both are stone pine forests. In addition, coastal pine forests were built starting from the early 20th century, mainly using maritime pine; today, they occupy a total area of about 850 hectares and represent an identifying landscape of the Ravenna area. Today the pine forests are a portion of the territory protected by landscape legislation. However, on the other hand, the same legislation does not limit itself to giving indications about the natural heritage but also about the architectural and artistic one.

In addition to the iconic and cultural identity, the landscape is a legislative matter today. Recognising the value of the natural context, both from a biological point of view and from an aesthetic point of view, makes it a system to be protected and regulated. However, the complexity of the legal matter regarding the issue of environmental protection is relatively high. As Prof. Stefano Grassi explains[39]:

> The concept of environment is a relational concept- transversal to all the other principles and values defined in the constitutional norms – which refers to at least three types of relationship:
>
> a) that between man and nature, with the possibility of defining the environment according to an anthropocentric conception ... which is opposed to an ecocentric conception .... From this point of view, the definition of environment invests choices that concern the ethical dimension of the relationship between man and nature…
> b) the diachronic and dynamic relationship that characterises ecosystems ...
> c) the relationship with the different territorial areas, with the possibility of having different problems depending on whether they are taken into consideration: the whole; biosphere; the regional areas; individual ecosystems.
>
> (Grassi, 2017)

The need for a definition of what landscape is a consequence of the recognition of the need for its protection. From a historical point of view, Italy holds the record for having included the concept of the environment in the founding articles of its Constitution. *Article 9 of the Italian Constitution*, drafted in 1948, stated: "The Republic promotes the development of culture and scientific and technical research"[40]. Furthermore, it protects the landscape and the historical and artistic heritage of the nation. A historical precedent can be found in the Constitution of the Weimar Republic of 1919, in Article 150: "Historic monuments, works of art, beauties of nature, and the Landscape are protected and cared for by the Reich"[41]. However, this does not fall within the founding articles of the Constitution.

Another antecedent to be pointed out is that of the Constitution of the Spanish Republic of 1931, which in article 45 reads:

> 1. Everyone has the right to use an environment suitable for the development of the person, as well as the duty to conserve it. 2. The public authorities will watch over the rational use of all-natural resources to protect and improve the quality of life and defend and restore the environment, relying on the indispensable collective solidarity.

Therefore, the indication of the Italian Constitution remains the first to express itself with the term landscape specifically in regard to its protection. Furthermore, an indication will be integrated in 2021 with attention to biodiversity and the ecosystem.

Finally, before introducing the current definitions of the landscape, it is essential to mention the Stockholm Declaration, which, in 1972, established for the first time at the European level the need to preserve the landscape. In the preamble, we read:

1. Man is both creature and creator of his environment, which assures him of his physical subsistence and offers him the possibility of an intellectual, moral, social and spiritual development…
2. The protection and improvement of the environment is a question of capital importance which concerns the well-being of peoples and the economic development of the whole world; it responds to the urgent desire of the peoples of the whole world and constitutes a duty for all governments.

In the principles, therefore, one can read that:

1. Man has a fundamental right to freedom, equality and satisfactory living conditions in an environment which allows him to live in dignity and well-being. He has a solemn duty to protect and improve the environment for the benefit of present and future generations.
2. The Earth's natural resources, including air, water, land, flora and fauna, and particularly representative samples of natural ecosystems, must be preserved in the interest of present and future generations through adequate planning and management.
3. The Earth's capacity to produce essential renewable resources must be maintained and, wherever possible, restored and enhanced.
4. Man is responsible for safeguarding and wisely managing the heritage of wild flora and fauna and their habitat, which are seriously threatened today by a combination of unfavourable factors. The conservation of nature, especially wild flora and fauna must therefore have an important place in planning for economic development.

Today, there are numerous definitions and laws dealing with the landscape. In order to give the measure of the importance of this field of investigation, we propose below a selection of the fundamental laws and the most important definitions.

Landscape Definitions

Landscape "*designa una determinata parte di territorio, così come è percepita dalle popolazioni, il cui carattere deriva dall'azione di fattori naturali e/o umani e dalle loro interrelazioni*". ["designates a certain part of the territory, as perceived by the populations, whose character derives from the action of natural and/or human factors and their interrelationships".]

(Convenzione Europea del Paesaggio, versione italiana, Capitolo 1, art. 1 lettera a)

Articolo 131 (Paesaggio). "*1. Per paesaggio si intende il territorio espressivo di identità, il cui carattere deriva dall'azione di fattori naturali, umani e dalle loro interrelazioni. 2. Il presente Codice tutela il paesaggio relativamente a quegli aspetti e caratteri che costituiscono rappresentazione materiale e visibile dell'identità nazionale, in quanto espressione di valori culturali*". ["By landscape we mean the expressive territory of identity, whose character derives from the action of natural and human factors and their interrelationships. 2. This Code protects the landscape in relation to those aspects and characteristics which constitute a material and visible representation of national identity, as an expression of cultural values".]

(Codice dei Beni Culturali e del Paesaggio) – Italia

" 'Landscape' is defined as a zone or area as perceived by local people or visitors, whose visual features and character are the result of the action of natural and/or cultural (that is, human) factors. This definition reflects the idea that landscapes evolve through time due to being acted upon by natural forces and human beings. It also underlines that a landscape forms a whole whose natural and cultural components are taken together, not separately".

Explanatory Report – ETS 176 – European Landscape Convention

Art 1.2. "*La tutela e la valorizzazione del patrimonio culturale concorrono a preservare la memoria della comunità nazionale e del suo territorio e a promuovere lo sviluppo della cultura*". [The protection and enhancement of cultural heritage contribute to preserving the memory of the national community and its territory and to promoting the development of culture.]

Art 2.1. "*Il patrimonio culturale e' costituito dai beni culturali e dai beni paesaggistici*". [Cultural heritage is made up of cultural assets and landscape assets.]

Art 2.2. "*Sono beni culturali le cose immobili e mobili che, ai sensi degli articoli 10 e 11, presentano interesse artistico, storico, archeologico, etnoantropologico, archivistico e bibliografico e le altre cose individuate dalla legge o in base alla legge quali testimonianze aventi valore di civiltà*". [Cultural assets are immovable and movable things which, pursuant to articles 10 and 11, have artistic, historical, archaeological, ethno-anthropological, archival and bibliographic interest and other things identified by law or on the basis of the law as evidence of civilizational value.]

Art 2.3. "*Sono beni paesaggistici gli immobili e le aree indicati all'articolo 134, costituenti espressione dei valori storici, culturali, naturali, morfologici ed estetici del territorio, e gli altri beni individuati dalla legge o in base alla legge*". [Landscape assets are the buildings and areas indicated in article 134, constituting an expression of the historical, cultural, natural, morphological and aesthetic values of the territory, and the other assets identified by law or on the basis of the law.]

Decreto legislativo 22 gennaio 2004, n. 42, in materia di "Codice dei beni culturali e del paesaggio, ai sensi dell'articolo 10 della legge 6 luglio 2002, n. 137" – Italia

"Landscape is about the relationship between people and place. It provides the setting for our day-to-day lives. The term does not mean just exceptional or designated landscapes; it does not only apply to the countryside. Landscape can mean a small patch of urban wasteland as much as a mountain range and an urban park as much as an expanse of lowland plain. It results from the way that different components of our environment – both natural (the influences of geology, soils, climate, flora and fauna) and cultural (the historical and current impact of land use, settlement, enclosure and other human interventions) – interact together and are perceived by us".

"Landscape Character Assessment: Guidance for England and Scotland (2002)", Scottish Natural Heritage and The Countryside Agency, p. 2

"The Landscape results from the subsurface and the functions that occur in an area, the use and the traces of this from the past. In the Netherlands, agriculture, using 60% of the space, is strongly its image. However, villages, towns and infrastructure are also strong images decisive. The scenery is what someone sees from one area, how he or she experiences it and with his or her senses it perceive. Also, sometimes invisible traces, such as archaeological places and geological elements, are part of it and stories. The Landscape contributes to the formation of local cultures. It forms an essential part of its natural and cultural heritage but also changes with time and our demands on our environment. In the Netherlands, twenty National landscapes have been designated to preserve and develop this heritage".

"Agenda Landscha", p. 8

Art 9. "*La Repubblica promuove lo sviluppo della cultura e la ricerca scientifica e tecnica. Tutela il paesaggio e il patrimonio storico e artistico della Nazione. Tutela l'ambiente, la biodiversità e gli ecosistemi, anche nell'interesse delle future generazioni. La legge dello Stato disciplina i modi e le forme di tutela degli animali*". [The Republic promotes the development of culture and scientific and technical research. It protects the landscape and the historical and artistic heritage of the nation. Protect the environment, biodiversity and ecosystems, also in the interest of future generations. State law regulates the methods and forms of animal protection.]

"Constitution of the Italian State"

"The Third Landscape – an undetermined fragment of the Planetary Garden – designates the sum of the space left over by man to landscape evolution – to nature alone. This category includes left-behind urban or rural sites, transitional spaces, neglected land, swamps, moors, peat bogs, roadsides, shores, railroad embankments, etc. To these isolated areas can be added space set aside, reserves in themselves: inaccessible places, mountain summits, non-cultivatable areas, deserts; institutional reserves: national parks, regional parks, and nature reserves".

Gilles Clement[42] – *The Third Landscape*

"So, in practice, landscape architects and park designers work in a realm between illusion and public policy, and our work is inevitably the banalest and compromised among the design disciplines. However, at the end of the day, are the built realities anywhere close to the dreamt-of parks and artists' impressions?"

Adriaan Geuze[43] and Matthew Skjonsberg[44], "Second Nature: New Territories for the Exiled" (2010)

"The picture took on fullness and density; it grew in structure and balance and came to maturity immediately. 'The landscape thinks itself in me,' he said, 'and I am its consciousness.' Nothing could be farther from naturalism than this intuitive science. Art is not imitation, nor is it something manufactured according to the wishes of instinct or good taste. It is a process of expressing".

Maurice Merleau-Ponty[45], *Cézanne's Doubt* (1945)

"1.Landscape is not a genre of art but a medium
2. Landscape is a medium of exchange between the human and the natural, the self and the other. As such, it is like money: good for nothing in itself but expressive of a potentially limitless reserve of value
3. Like money, Landscape is a social hieroglyph that conceals the actual basis of its value. It does so by naturalising its conventions and conventionalising its Nature
4. Landscape is a natural scene mediated by culture. It is both a represented and presented space, both a signifier and a signified, both a frame and what a frame contains, both a real place and its simulacrum, and both a package and the commodity inside the package
5. Landscape is a medium found in all cultures
6. Landscape is a particular historical formation associated with European imperialism
7. Theses 5 and 6 do not contradict one other

8. Landscape is an exhausted medium, no longer viable as a mode of artistic expression. Like life, Landscape is boring; we must not say so
9. The Landscape referred to in Thesis 8 is the same as that of Thesis 6".

William J. Thomas Mitchell[46], *Landscape and Power* (1994)

"When the environment is something more than a group of factors and parameters, when we sometimes enjoy the Landscape or Nature just as merchandise, when we talk about tourism or about natural parks as theme parks, when we talk about the forgotten landscapes of the outskirts…has not the ideas changed enough in its use, the values and management of the ground so that have to give a new name to the elements of the Landscape, the tools to contemplate it, or to make it?"

Rosa Barba i Casanovas[47], *Designing… In which Landscape?* (2010)

ACT 5: OUTDOOR FACILITIES ACTUAL DEFINITION

Given what has been illustrated so far, it is time to clarify what an accommodation facility for outdoor tourism is and how it distinguishes itself. However, first, it should be explained that there is no unique European definition from a regulatory point of view, so we will give a generic definition and collect the indications of some European countries where open-air tourism is more widespread.

Open-air accommodation facilities usually arise in locations characterised by particular environmental and natural qualities (sea, lakes and mountains) that are the main attraction for visitors. These "holiday cities" (Trillo, 2003) have some common foundational traits that remain immanent despite the temporality of their use:

- Each accommodation facility is defined by a **perimeter**, variable in its materialisation. This dividing line can consist of a wall, a metal fence or even just plant elements (i.e. a hedge); it tends to be opaque or obscured to maintain privacy. Crossing the border to access the internal space of the accommodation facility and the activities included therein is generally exclusive to those staying in the facility;
- There is always a system of stable **services**, built using different technologies, which host functions and services for users: a reception, restaurants, sports activities, commercial activities and recreational activities;
- There is a system of **temporary living system**. These fittings have the common trait of removability, whether owned by the user (the tourist), such as campers, caravans or tents, or owned by the structure or external operators, such as Maxi-Caravans.

Open-air accommodation facilities are, by their very nature, characterised by a landscape of substantial value. The natural environment offered to tourists is safe, aesthetically defined and comfortable both from a point of view of perception and use. The landscape built or maintained within these places becomes iconic of the place itself, sometimes even identifying a specific region or territory.

If campsite is a common and shared idea, in the act of a holiday in nature, its standardisation is specific to each state in which it is regulated. However, the Italian case illustrates the dimension of the non-specificity of campsite, which is defined region by region. In Italy, outdoor tourism covers a large part of tourism in general, in which landscape protection is exceptionally necessary, as expressed in previous pages. As already illustrated in the general introduction to this discussion, the value of open-air tourism as an economic sector is expanding and must be accompanied by a reflection on its environmental impact, not only from an efficiency point of view but also from a cultural point of view.

Italy is also, along with France, the country with the most significant number of assets (7 out of a total of 98) belonging to the transversal category of cultural landscapes, introduced in 1992. Cultural landscapes, defined as the "combined result of work of nature and man", are those that "reflect specific land use techniques that ensure and sustain biological diversity" or are "associated in the perception of communities with beliefs and customs of artistic or traditional value"[48]. It is also important to underline the recognition of the value of the landscape as an Italian artistic heritage to be valorised, as stated in Article 24 of the Italian Tourism Code:

> Incentivazione di iniziative di promozione turistica finalizzate alla valorizzazione del patrimonio storico – artistico, archeologico, architettonico e paesaggistico italiano – 1. Nel rispetto dell'articolo 9 della Costituzione e del codice dei beni culturali e del paesaggio di cui al decreto legislativo 22 gennaio 2004, n. 42, il Presidente del Consiglio dei Ministri o il Ministro delegato, di concerto con il Ministro per i beni e le attività culturali, promuove la realizzazione di iniziative turistiche finalizzate ad incentivare la valorizzazione del patrimonio storico – artistico, archeologico, architettonico e paesaggistico presente sul territorio italiano, utilizzando le risorse umane e strumentali disponibili, senza nuovi ed ulteriori oneri per la finanza pubblica.[49] [Encouragement of tourism promotion initiatives aimed at enhancing the Italian historical – artistic, archaeological, architectural and landscape heritage – 1. In compliance with article 9 of the Constitution and the code of cultural heritage and landscape referred to in the legislative decree of 22 January 2004, n. 42, the President of the Council of Ministers or the delegated Minister, in agreement with the Minister for Cultural Heritage and Activities, promotes the implementation of tourist initiatives aimed at promoting the valorisation of the historical-artistic, archaeological, architectural and landscape heritage present on the territory. Italian territory, using available human and instrumental resources, without new and additional burdens on public finances.]

Even Italy, however, does not have a single standard at the national level but leaves the definition of the limits concerning campsite activities to the individual regions (and sometimes to the municipalities). With the legislative decree 79/2011, the government has definitively launched the Tourism Code to promote the tourism market and strengthen consumer protection. Article 13 is the one linked explicitly to accommodation facilities for outdoor tourism. Point 5 says:

1. For the purposes of this legislative decree, as well as for the purposes of exercising state administrative power referred to in article 15, the following are open-air accommodation facilities: a) tourist villages; b) campsites; c) campsites as part of agritourism activities; d) holiday parks.
2. Tourist villages are accommodation facilities open to the public, with unitary management, set up and equipped in fenced-off areas intended for the rest and stay of tourists in minimum setups, mainly without their own overnight accommodation means.
3. Tourist villages may also have campsite pitches equipped for the rest and stay of tourists with their own mobile means of overnight accommodation.
4. Campsites are accommodation facilities open to the public, with unitary management, set up and equipped on fenced-off areas intended for the rest and stay of tourists mainly with their own mobile means of overnight accommodation. The term campsite can be used as an alternative to the term campsite.
5. **Campsites may also have mobile housing units, such as tents, caravans or caravans, mobile-homes or maxi caravans, motor homes or campers, and fixed housing units, for the stopover and stay of tourists without their mobile means of overnight.**
6. Campsites in the context of agritourism activities are open-air reception areas managed by agricultural entrepreneurs by the law of 20 February 2006, n. 96, containing the regulation of agritourism.
7. Campsites with unified management are holiday parks in which pitches are rented to a single crew for the entire duration of the structure's opening period.
8. Open-air accommodation facilities are classified based on the requirements and characteristics according to the prescriptions established by the regions and autonomous provinces of Trento and Bolzano.

9. In the outdoor accommodation facilities, the following are ensured: a) continuous surveillance of the accommodation facility during the opening periods; b) the continuous presence within the accommodation facility of the manager or his delegate; c) insurance coverage for civil liability risks in favour of customers.

Therefore, the standard dedicated to outdoor accommodation distinguishes between tourist villages and campsites in the context of agritourism activities and holiday parks. The common trait of these structures is the enclosure, which defines their boundaries and establishes their ownership, with consequent responsibilities. From the point of view of the Tourism Code, the distinction between tourist villages and campsites is very subtle and depends on the service rendered rather than the structure.

While tourist villages are aimed at tourists "mainly without their own means of overnight accommodation", the campsites are "accommodation structures open to the public, with unitary management, set up and equipped in fenced areas intended for the rest and stay of tourists, mainly equipped with their own means of accommodation[50]". The distinction between campsites and tourist villages, therefore, is based on the criterion of the orientation of the touristic offer to those who arrive already equipped with their means to stay and sleep (a camper, a caravan or a tent) or to those who do not have it and, therefore, will have to use the housing solutions made available by the structure. However, the distinction is subtle because it is based on the criterion of the prevalence of tourists with or without these own means, and it is possible for the managers to "mix" the offers and availability of places in the dedicated areas. Moreover, the law provides that even tourist villages can "have campsite pitches equipped for the rest and stay of tourists with their mobile overnight accommodation"[51]. Furthermore, the introduction of the mobile home product further complicates this distinction, given that this can be positioned on "free" pitches in a mainly autonomous way.

Similar indications can be found, for example, in the regulation of the Veneto Region, one of the most important in terms of the number of entries linked to this type of tourism.

<u>Art. 26 – Outdoor accommodation facilities – REGIONAL LAW n. 11 of 14 June 2013</u>

1. Open-air accommodation facilities are open to the public, with unitary management, which offers tourists, in an enclosed area, accommodation in mobile set-ups or housing units divided into tourist villages and campsites.
2. Set-ups for overnight stays in the open-air accommodation facility, installed on specific pitches by the owner of the accommodation facility or by tourists, such as tents, caravans, campers, caravans and mobile homes, are considered mobile installations.
3. Tourist villages are open-air accommodation facilities with total or prevalent accommodation capacity in housing units or mobile installations installed by the owner and with any residual accommodation capacity in mobile installations installed by tourists.
4. Campsites or campsites are open-air accommodation facilities with total or prevalent accommodation capacity in mobile installations installed by tourists and any residual accommodation capacity in housing units or mobile installations installed by the owner.
5. Open-air accommodation facilities are required to ensure:

   a) continuous surveillance of the accommodation facility during the opening periods;
   b) the presence, on an ongoing basis, within the accommodation facility of the owner or his delegate.

The Tuscany region specifies the concept of prevalence in more detail by adding a numerical quantification:

> Art. 31[52] – Areas of the structure (art. 3, paragraph 1, letter l) and art. 17, paragraph 3, letter c) of the regional law 86/2016)
>
> 2. The complex of areas intended for services and those free for common use can be at least 10 per cent of the entire pertinent area of the structure, excluding surfaces intended for internal roads.

Furthermore, regional law 86/2016 (consolidated text of the regional tourism system) innovated the discipline of tourism, replacing the previous "consolidated text of regional laws on tourism", i.e. regional law 42/2000, which was by then an inadequate tool, despite having been subject to modifications over the years.

For campsites, the definition of a structure temporarily anchored to the ground has been superseded concerning compliance with urban planning and construction and, where applicable, landscape requirements. Furthermore, the manager is allowed to offer (in addition to 40% of mobile homes) tents and related accessories owned by the manager for a further 20% of the pitches. Where the structures temporarily anchored to the ground account for more than 30% of the pitches, the campsite can be called a "campsite village". For campsites, there is the possibility – as for hotels – to exercise activities for those who need to be accommodated.

The regulation of the Lombardy region adds information about the elements of the campsite without distinguishing between campsites and tourist villages:

a) pitch: the equipped area reserved for the exclusive use of one or more people staying together;
b) fixed housing units: fittings fixed stably to the ground;
c) mobile housing units: fittings not permanently tied to the ground and mobile overnight accommodation units;
d) accessories and appurtenances of mobile housing units: light manufactured articles placed in the specific pitches by the owners of the accommodation facilities or by tourists, which can be removed at any time and in any case no later than the deadline set for the use of the pitch, such as veranda-tents, systems permeable shading, covers to protect the mobile housing units and the relative veranda, raised platforms outside the mobile housing units, pre-entrances with structure made of rigid or semi-rigid materials, which can be disassembled and transported in any case, to be combined with the mobile housing units, with protection and day stay of people.

To sum up, campsites and tourist villages fall into the "accommodation facilities for outdoor tourism" category. This belonging of theirs is linked to focusing most of the space and activities in the open space. They are characterised by an enclosure, which defines their ownership, limits and responsibilities according to the users and the space itself. They can host users with their equipment or provide their equipment. The open space dedicated to the reception of tourists is organised in pitches. These are the essence of campsite, as they are the accommodations that gave rise to outdoor holidays. Therefore, the pitches' surface varies in size and type: gravel to grass, synthetic grass or other more extravagant solutions. For other services, on the other hand, the pitch can be either "surface only" or supplied with electricity and/or water connections.

The housing units provided by the structure can be of two types: the bungalows, which are tiny stable homes, and the Maxi-Caravan or mobile homes, which are removable housing units. Of these two categories, the first complies with the standard Italian building regulations. Therefore, it represents a real construction to all intents and purposes, while the second falls into the "mobile equipment" category. This distinction should be compared with the fact that most campsites in Italy are located in areas that must be defined as sensitive. These are areas of high landscape and naturalistic value where building is usually completely forbidden. Many of the accommodation facilities for open-air tourism were built (with the appropriate permit) before the definition of these areas and the constraints that characterise them today.

The cultural heritage code identifies the **areas of landscape interest**[53]**:**

a) the coastal territories included in a depth band of 300 meters from the shoreline, even for elevated land above the sea;
b) the territories adjacent to the lakes included in a strip of a depth of 300 meters from the shoreline, also for the territories elevated on the lakes;
c) the rivers, streams, and watercourses registered in the lists envisaged by the consolidated text of the provisions of the law on water and electrical systems, approved by Royal Decree of 11 December 1933, n. 1775, and the relative banks or feet of the embankments for a strip of 150 meters each;
d) mountains for the part exceeding 1,600 meters above sea level for the Alpine chain and 1,200 meters above sea level for the Apennine chain and for the islands;
f) national or regional parks and reserves, as well as the external protection territories of the parks;
g) territories covered by forests and woods, even if traversed or damaged by fire, and those subject to reforestation restrictions, as defined by article 2, paragraphs 2 and 6, of legislative decree 18 May 2001, n. 227.

Given the clarification of this legislative dimension, it is easy to understand why mobile homes are spreading throughout the Italian territory. Their removability and ability to be positioned without serious bureaucratic procedures (Berizzi and Trabattoni, 2019 determine their popularity. On the other hand, the positioning of a mobile home, in its technical simplicity, however, involves rethinking the landscape.

Maxi-Caravan Landscape

The landscape within open-air accommodation facilities is a matter of little depth. From a commercial point of view, the simple nomenclature "in the open air" guarantees a specific type of user. This same user, however, mainly since the pandemic but not solely during this timeframe, is changing "tastes".

Compared to tents or caravans and trailers, the Maxi-Caravan raises the level of expectations in terms of comfort and services provided. Furthermore, the rules on respect for the landscape often impose limits about architecture as well. If the urban constraints on construction are easily identifiable, in built contexts, relationships and the environment, they become vaguer. In rural contexts, reference is made to the recovery of the characteristics of agricultural architecture, which is also protected in Italy. In contexts with a solid naturalistic value, where it is forbidden to build, when it is allowed, reference is made to materials and colours. The result is a reflection on the landscape that considers mobile homes in an integrated way.

In a traditional open-air tourist accommodation facility, the landscape aspect is given by the concurrence of three factors: the prevalence of empty space with respect to the built-up area; the presence of natural elements, often artificial, such as pine forests, explicitly created to protect agricultural land from the influence of the sea and which have now become a symbolic and characteristic element of the Italian coasts; and the presence of a prevailing landscape, usually the first vehicle of attraction for tourists. However, the insertion of the "mobile home", unlike the tent or caravan, implies the positioning of an artificial structure, which for the duration of the industrial product's life, will participate in the vision of the internal landscape of the campsite. Even if for a limited period of the holiday, the perception of the space of the accommodation facility will be linked to the presence of the housing units, and therefore their inclusion in a landscaped context becomes significant according to the quality of the perceived space.

Furthermore, let us consider that mobile homes can be positioned anywhere, but that campsites are not designed for mobile homes. The contingency of landscape construction design linked to these settlements becomes evident.

The design process would be linear if the campsite were built from scratch. However, the reality of the facts, at least in Italy, is that campsites have experienced a constant increase over the last 50 years, usually without planning, most of the time as a sequence of additions without coherence. A list of graphic translations of 20 campsites is now being proposed to highlight the extent of this change, which diagrammatically highlights the variation experienced from the date of foundation to today.

The Settlement System (Graphic Results of the "Mobile Home" Research Coordinated with AUDe Laboratory of the University of Pavia)

The work developed within the AUDe laboratory of the University of Pavia is based on various sources. As the research on the history of the campsite has tried to illustrate, these accommodation facilities are often born informally and are family-run. Unfortunately, the paper documentation concerning the historical evolution of the structures, which has seen land acquisitions and changes in the accommodation units, is often absent. A reconnaissance of photographic sources has been carried out to obtain this information, starting from the historical satellite images. Unfortunately, however, even these cover a limited time. The change in open-air accommodation facilities is shown with the oldest available date (when possible, that of the start of the activity). Finally, this situation is compared with that of the survey, i.e. 2020.

When it was impossible to recover official iconographic material, open-source tools were used, allowing a satellite view of the past. The date of the plans is deduced from the sources. The comparison with the situation is, however, very significant since it shows the expansion of the structures and the construction of the complex landscape described up to now, giving excellent value to the need for its planning. The graphic reworkings represent a synthesis of the typological elements that characterise the campsite to analytically highlight the relationship between natural elements and permanent and mobile structures. Above the schematic redesign of the road structure of the campsite, which shows roads and pitches, the identified elements are those that have already been described in this discussion:

- Maxi-Caravan
- Tents, campers, caravans (identified in shape concerning the space occupied)
- Permanent structures
- Tree-lined fabric
- Intensive green

The link below shows the result of this work, noting how the actual development of these temporary settlements is increasing both in the dimensions of the settlements and in the amount of maxi-caravan settled down. Just as a clarification, in this work it is possible to see the previous diagram of Camping Village Cavallino situated in Cavallino Treporti near Venice in Italy. This campsite has grown in the last 60 years from *8ha* to *13ha* adding more or less *400* Maxi-Caravans.

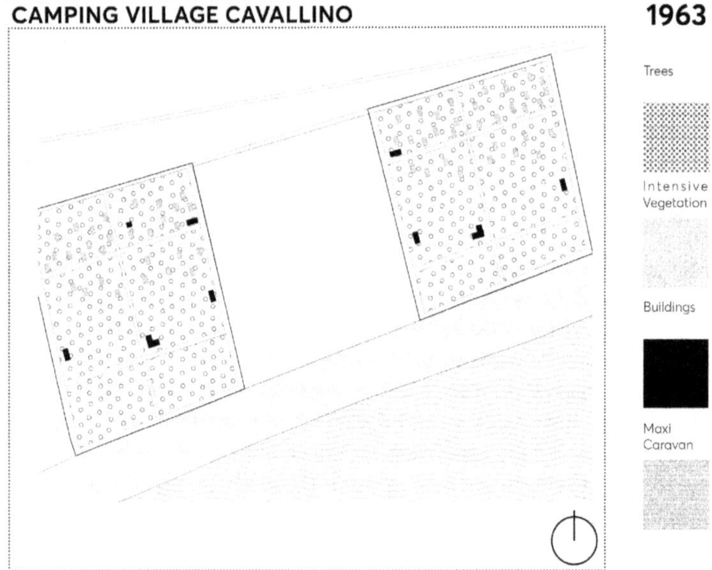

Figure 2.8 Camping Village Cavallino 1963

To see the whole graphic work see the link: https://www.campdesign.it/campsite-research.

Strategies for Campsite Development

The Maxi-Caravan is at the centre of a revolution in open-air tourism, which includes rethinking the way of holidaying. In the period following the pandemic, interest in open-air holidays has increased.

> The general perception is that the current situation has influenced the appeal towards accommodation facilities in the Outdoor world: the desire to be in contact with nature and attention to safety are two elements that have married very well in the 2020 summer season and have led people to perceive Outdoor solutions positively. Furthermore, the pandemic has helped to underline, in the eyes of travellers, some peculiar characteristics of the Outdoor accommodation categories, such as large spaces, immersion in nature and independent accommodation solutions[54].

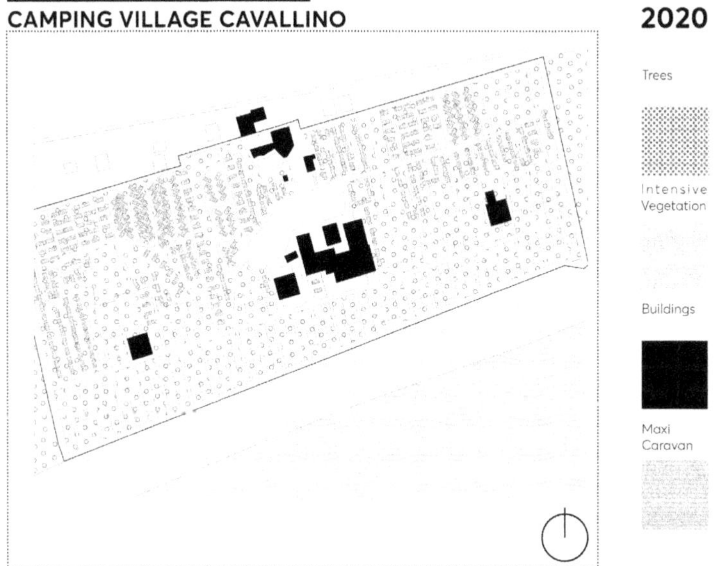

Figure 2.9 Camping Village Cavallino 2020

The market response to tourist presence is linked to the attempt to translate users' wishes. These desires focus on three macro-themes: *sustainability*, *experientiality* and *comfort*.

In recent years, the growth of awareness around environmental issues and a new ecological culture, factors present above all in the European context, have broadened the concept of "respect for nature" by making explicit values that go far beyond the aesthetic factor and involve more substantial issues, such as: the impact of our actions on the environment; the protection and promotion of landscapes and biodiversity; the reduction of the consumption of non-renewable resources; and the reduction of sources of pollution. Moreover, in the face of a planetary need, sustainability has become a full-blown necessity from a commercial point of view, induced by more aware and demanding tourists.

The central issues in this respect are certainly the maintenance of the habitat in order to compensate for the tourist impact. This phenomenon is called Overtourism, which unbalances the human impact on the context. However, more than the natural element, albeit aesthetically prevalent, is needed. There are undoubtedly organisational factors to consider, such as waste and resource management. There are also energy issues. In this panorama, the Maxi-Caravan industrial product takes advantage of its installation system, which does not require foundations and is highly removable. These characteristics are a factor in the idea of non-consumption of land. This feature, combined with a product development consistent with sustainability, and therefore calibrated on materials and construction technologies and thermal management, enhances its use. The Maxi-Caravan can be read as an ecological system of comfort for inhabiting the natural landscape.

Within the tourism sector, another factor that has become decisive is that of the experientiality of the holiday, or the ability to convey a sense of uniqueness and exclusivity. There are many strategies to achieve this goal, starting from the communication of the structure up to the qualification of the context. The study of the aesthetic aspect of the structure is part of the enhancement of the visual communication linked to the holiday experience, what Jhon Urry has defined as the *Tourist Gaze* (Urry, 2002).

The *Tourist Gaze* can be built in two ways: internally, through the decoding that the tourist carries out based on his socio-cultural filters, and externally, by professionals in the sector who create an image of the tourist product that will influence the tourist's expectations. Experientiality, therefore, arises before the actual period of the holiday, and the concept of the *Tourist Gaze* contributes to the construction of expectations about the uniqueness of the holiday. Again, the mutability of the landscape, while maintaining some essential characteristics, becomes a qualifying value of open-air accommodation facilities. The construction of the landscape that follows the installation of the mobile home, and in concert, the timing of renewal induced by the characteristics of the industrial product, must be read as potential within the experientiality of tourism.

The construction of mobile home clusters involves defining stable elements (secular trees, land morphology, panoramic views) and other changeable ones (paths, small trees, low vegetation, lighting). These two variables, combined with the mutability of the housing object, generate a large sequence of variables. In this way, tourism times work on two levels: the "long" time, i.e. that of the industrial product (7 years), guarantees renewal; the short time (that of the tourist, the summer season) guarantees affiliation. This oscillation between "domestic" and "exotic" allows the outdoor facilities structures to respond to the tourist's gaze.

The quality of the accommodation is the factor most linked to the development of the Maxi-Caravan industrial product. Furthermore, the search for an almost domestic spatiality is the tool to enhance the perception of luxury, especially concerning caravans and trailers. The legislation that defines these spatialities is linked to the characteristics of the industrial product. The housing dimensions are, in fact, much smaller than domestic ones and are close to those of means of transport. The idea of domesticity, however, is sought by pursuing the image and privacy of domestic spaces. The Maxi-Caravans are always organised traditionally, with one or two closable bedrooms (maximum size 6m^2), a kitchen, a table for eating, two or more bathrooms and a living area. All functions are reduced beyond the minimum in size. However, the element that best qualifies the housing units is the external space or the covered veranda. This space, created in continuity with the units, is a valid extension of the internal space. The openings of the houses, often developed on one side only, always face the verandas. These spaces, shaded and covered, define the spatial filter alongside the collective dimension of the campsite; it is a technical connection system. The Maxi-Caravans are positioned with their transport trolley, which necessitates a step of about 60cm from the ground. This leap is solved by using external stairs integrated into the verandas. Mobile homes represent a compromise between the dream of a house in the middle of nature and a mass holiday.

The phenomenon of glamping represents the latest embodiment of this aspiration. The definition of glamour campsite is linked to a vision of this type of open-air holiday, but one designed with high levels of luxury and isolation. The quality of the accommodation is very high, even when it comes to tents rather than mobile homes. The endowment of internal and offered services joins a settlement system that favours isolation and a low density of units in nature. If there is a historical reference to this approach to holidays, it can be found in extraordinary situations not related to tourism. The famous *Field of the Cloth of Gold (Camp du Drap d'Or)*[55], mentioned in relation to this experience, is indicative because it summarises the theme of exaggerated luxury applied to a temporary accommodation system based on tents. The Campo del Drappo d'Oro was the site of the famous meeting between Francis I and Henry VIII, King of England. It owes its name to the splendour with which the two rival powers competed. Henry's palace covered nearly 2.5 acres (1 hectare) and was sumptuously decorated; it contained a great hall and a spacious chapel, and, outside, a sparkling fountain spouted claret, hippocras (spiced wine) and water through separate runlets.

Even in informal contexts today, the idea of luxury intertwines with the idea of isolation, clearly understood with to denote exclusivity. This definition leads to carefully rereading many of the campsites that open areas defined as "glamping". In these cases, the difference between them and the "village" areas, i.e., developed using mobile homes, is often minimal. If glamping, therefore, remains a luxury service, the mobile home is instead a mass transformation. Due to its diffusion, it redefines the approach to planning open-air tourist structures, considering the presence of these industrial products as a foundation.

Clustering and Landscape Construction

Few manuals explain how to plan a campsite settlement. However, one of the most famous manuals in tourism planning is Inskeep's one. This manual talks about tourism management, but also gives some instructions about settlements. Thomas Inskeep's *Tourist Planning* places the campsite among extraordinary tourist activities and introduces some settlement strategies. A transversal reading of the manual allows us to draw some considerations, starting from application systems not explicitly related to campsite—for example, reflections on the vegetation and the organisation of the housing units. Inskeep proposes a series of standards that must be considered in the development of tourist facilities, some of which are also applicable to campsites:

> The density of development, Setbacks of buildings for amenity features, shorelines, roads, lot lines, and other buildings coverage of the site by buildings and other structures other requirements such as landscaping and open space, public access to amenity features, signs and utility lines.
>
> (Inskeep, 1991, p. 310)

Specifically, it shows the relationship between infrastructure, housing units and landscape. The first approach deals with low density. It develops a few units connected by a sinuous infrastructure, referring to a hypothetical immersion in the landscape. The second example makes the number of units more dense in relation to the development of the infrastructure, reading the street as a place for sharing. The third works on unifying multiple units around clusters of empty (equipped) space to enhance the relations between tourists; the infrastructure becomes a service that connects several "squares".

> The grouping of buildings, such as accommodation and their relationships to amenity and recreation facilities, is an essential concern of site planning. The type of grouping depends on the density and character of development desired as related to the natural environment.
>
> (Inskeep, 1991, p. 305)

In this first approach, linked to the relationship between the housing units, Inskeep follows some reflections on the relationship between the housing units and the "amenities". In the context of the campsite, the amenities coincide with the "prevailing landscape", i.e. the landscape system of reference (sea, mountains, lake, etc.). Inskeep's reflections concern the possibility of maintaining the visual relationship between all the units and the landscape, positioning the various rows of housing units in an offset or inclined manner.

> Another important consideration…is the maintenance of views or at least view corridors toward amenity features…the location, height and orientation of buildings should be controlled so that view planes of distant features such as mountains or sea are maintained.
>
> (Inskeep, 1991, p. 309)

The campsite is also included as an example in the *Architect's Data* manual by Neufert in its chapter on accommodation[56]. Neufert's indications are specific and functional concerning the accessibility and management of services. While specifying the sizing of the areas and roads according to the services and quantities, Neufert does not define real settlement systems. The proposed settlement scheme reflects on the relationship between the road, understood as a driveway, as the primary circulation system, and empty areas (space for housing units). The comparison between these models and the current world of the campsite (as seen in the visual analysis of Italian campsite sites) involves a reflection on the perception of the landscape. Suppose it is true that the "prevailing landscape" remains an essential reference for open-air accommodation facilities. In that case, it is also true that an extensive organisation of the campsite involves differentiation of the areas. In structures the size of several hectares, the relationship with the prevailing landscape, in fact, changes between the first line and the last. However, being structures codified on the relationship with the landscape, the construction of the landscape becomes a priority when linked to the settlement system. Significantly, if defined according to mobile homes and Maxi-Caravans, which provide for more extended periods, the relationship between units and units with external space deserves specific study.

The external space of the campsite is built by composing known elements and organising the mobile homes. The well-known elements are landscape architecture, i.e. flooring, paths, seats, outdoor lighting, vegetation and signage, and micro-architectures such as gazebos, canopies and covered walkways. The projects illustrated during the ECCE 2022 conference show how the architectural approach to the landscape, linked to known elements, can lead to solutions suitable for different contexts (Berizzi, *et al.*, 2023).

As already illustrated at the ISUF 2022[57] conference, it is possible to gather some intervention strategies in the campsite, beginning with a fundamental assumption that we will call "clustering". With this word, we want to define an approach to organising housing units that presupposes an organisation based on repeatable elements. The construction of these elements, or clusters, generates a settlement matrix that allows us to deal with the space of the accommodation facility. The cluster becomes the spatial reference of the users but also the generative system of the landscape. When we talk about clusters, we usually refer to a sector of housing units comprising three to six units. This approach for contained groups makes it possible to reduce the perceptive scale of the intervention, referring to a "vernacular" housing dimension, that which recalls the idea of a village. Furthermore, the cluster determines a reference landscape independent from the prevailing one. Therefore, the qualification of the open space contiguous to several mobile homes involves the construction of landscaped sections that live independently of the external context (the cluster). By proceeding in this way, without renouncing the perception of the starting context, it is possible to intervene in open-air accommodation structures, even those of large dimensions or far from the prevailing landscape.

As in the urban planning examples linked to ecology and greenery, the relationship between built and empty space is fundamental. The settlement strategies already illustrated during the ISUF conference are therefore re-proposed. All three combine the management of the housing units (Maxi-Caravans) with the landscape of the cluster and the perception of the prevailing landscape. This ternary system effectively responds to the time factor of the "medium time city".

The revolution of the urban landscape of open-air accommodation facilities can take place without distorting the general sector, adapting to both technical (Neufert) and market and ecological needs.

The theme of ecology is included in these strategies only when foundational. i.e. orientation, response to a specific orography and respect for the land or response to a persistent climatic condition (wind); even if of great value, the production potential linked to open spaces (such as phytodepuration systems, electricity production, water recovery) are not taken into consideration only because they are an addition to other settlement principles. They must therefore be understood as accessories, even if ethically essential.

Topographic Development

This approach strategy is applied in contexts where the landscape element predominates, so as to constrain the positioning of the housing units. This situation can occur for a particularly defined terrain reading and particular environmental conditions. An example could be seen in the case of terraced land, which represents a binding orographic situation..

In these situations, the conformation of the ground, being anthropised, is already developed according to a predominant view. The prevailing landscape, therefore, has a double subsistence: panoramic, which gives the reason for the direction of the terrain, and morphological, since the steps themselves are now a landscape with a recognised identity. In these situations, the morphological situation constrains the settlement principle of the houses, which, with a few variations, are positioned on the steps directing the main view towards the slope. The access systems follow the terrain, developing independently for each step.

COMMON SETTLEMENT SYSTEM

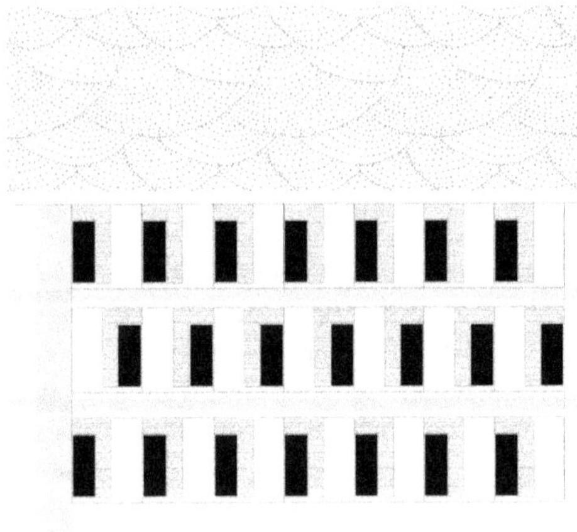

FOLLOWING INSKEEP'S IDEAS ABOUT SETTLEMENTS, THE LIVING UNITS ARE SETTLED DOWN TO EMPHASISE THE VIEW OF THE PREVALENT LANDSCAPE.
THE SECOND LINE IS MOVED TO OBTAIN A SIMILAR VIEW AS THE FIRST LINE.
STARTING FROM THE THIRD LINE, THE OTHER HOUSES BLOCK THE VIEW.
THIS SYSTEM OCCUPIES ALL THE SPACES.
THE PITCHES ARE FIXED ON A DIMENSION OF 150M2
THE HOUSES HAVE DIMENSIONS OF 10X4 MT, AND THEY HAVE AN EXTERNAL SPACE IN FRONT OF BOTH THE TWO MAIN SIDES

Figure 2.10 Common Settlement System Diagram

The settlement approach favours the panoramic relationship with the prevailing landscape, renouncing the connections between the housing units, which in this way can enjoy a greater sense of isolation. This settlement system that follows the orography according to the panoramic view of the living space is typical, for example, of glamping situations where the first necessity is isolation or a sense of uniqueness.

Another strong environmental constraint can be linked to the reading of persistent climatic conditions. Two examples of these conditions are the case of strong winds or unfortunate orientations. Especially in coastal situations, persistent winds can cause the deterioration of housing units and damage public space. A house facing the sea must deal with the difficulties associated with the climate, wind and saltiness. Given the campsite's primary condition, i.e., being in a fenced area, often being on the seafront does not guarantee an authentic sea view. In these cases, the prevailing landscape is a perceived presence and a service of proximity. Therefore, the settlement system can be an obstacle to the main natural element (winds), generating a mono-oriented housing system that protects the open space. In the

Figure 2.11 Topographic System

second example, it is possible to build meeting spaces and, therefore, not give up the collective dimension, but the size of these spaces will be balanced by the need to protect them. This approach brings together several elements and adds to other reflections; for example, positioning the houses must not make one give up the scaling factor, i.e., the clustering principle. In this case, the clusters will be oriented to the landscape/climate constraint, but will still be present.

Introverted Development

In most Italian campsites, the settlement size is such that the areas within the accommodation structure differ significantly in their relationship with external factors. Furthermore, landscape protection regulations push towards increasingly contingent buffer zones today[58]. This regulatory condition requires a reflection on the value of the landscape of open-air accommodation facilities regardless of the prevailing landscape. Furthermore, open-air accommodation facilities cover areas of several hectares, within which it may be appropriate to define different areas. This methodology of approach then proceeds to the definition of an autonomous and independent landscape linked explicitly to the Maxi-Caravan system.

The issue of clustering is crucial in this case. The introverted cluster comprises a variable, but reduced, number of housing units, which form a recognisable and compact nucleus. The perceived space is balanced between the private dimension (internal and external), linked to the development of the terraces or verandas of the houses, and the collective/aggregative one contained between the houses. The value of cluster closure is mainly determined by the high level of privacy it guarantees. The idea of security, especially in family contexts, characterises this approach, as well as that of identifiability. The use of the landscape, understood as a composition of artificial and natural houses and vegetation, builds the cluster's identity. There is an evident affinity with the settlement systems of prehistoric villages or pre-walled cities. This similarity is the idea of a small community whose living context is defined not by a fence but by the position of the housing units. As in the wagon circles of North American caravans, the size of the individual used protectively is aggregated to generate the size of the community.

Even if it is not correct to speak of community, to the extent of the relational relationships that can exist in a situation such as a holiday, the potential of this aggregative strategy lies in the possible and non-binding relationships. Therefore, the aggregation of a few people is privileged, generating internal contexts that may or may not dialogue with each other. The passage between the private and the collective dimension is mediated by architecture. For example, the covered or uncovered verandas represent a private space open to the outside. The quality and characteristics of the interstitial space between the units will determine the quality of the cluster. The composition of this internal landscape will be decisive. A tree or dense vegetation system in the centre will also generate distance between the cluster of houses, increasing privacy; a meeting place in the middle will define the space as a square (thematic, for example, as a play space for children). The housing units define the fence, a border that can be crossed but not welcomed, which isolates without separating. The variables in constructing the internal landscape must consider the current debate regarding landscape and sustainability:

- Valuing local essences has the double advantage of adapting to the local habitat and referring to the prevailing landscape.
- Use sustainable materials that facilitate rainwater drainage, whether recycled or recyclable or natural objects.

INTROVERTED/ENCLOSURE SYSTEM

THE UNITS CAN BE ORGANISED IN SMALL CLUSTERS THAT CAN BE REPEATED
THE FIRST LINE CAN BE MAINTAINED TO GET THE BEST VIEW OF THE PREVALENT LANDSCAPE.
THE LIVING UNITS BEHIND THE FIRST LINE DENY THE VIEW OF THE PRIMARY LANDSCAPE TO OBTAIN AN INTERNAL SITUATION.
THE HOUSES ARE ORGANISED IN SMALL GROUPS THAT CAN GENERATE SAFER PLACES FOR CHILDREN.
THE COMMON SPACE REDUCES PRIVACY BUT ALLOWS THE HOUSES TO HAVE MORE AIR AND LIGHT IN FRONT OF THEM.

Figure 2.12 Introverted System

- Introduce active water recycling and cleaning (constructed wetlands), exploiting renewable energies (wind, solar) and passive temperature mitigation systems.

Directed Development

An alternative to the system of introverted clusters may be to orient the clusters towards a specific direction, different from that of the prevailing landscape. This approach methodology starts by defining a new prevailing landscape alternative to the main one. For example, in a context such as the Italian one, where the degradation of the coasts and the erosion of the strip near the sea are incipient, the idea of lessening the use of these areas becomes primary. In these cases, it is possible, for example, to replicate the prevailing landscape, not so much in its physical characteristics, but rather in its use.

The example of the beach, rather than the long lake, refers to the informal use of a context in the open air. The degree of informality depends on the management of the property itself, but the potential remains active. This new landscape will shift the attention from the use and perception of the prevailing one, becoming the identity of a portion of the open-air accommodation facility, if not the whole. The settlement system of the cluster can therefore be developed, considering the new landscape as a reference point. The repeatability of the cluster will be related to the size of the new landscape. This space for collective use can be dedicated to the new sector or the entire structure. However, the proximity of the cluster system will make it exclusive. The clusters developed in this way will sacrifice part of the aggregative spatiality and, if possible, enhance the mobile homes' position to favour the landscape's perception. A horseshoe or U-shaped system open towards the landscape clarifies this settlement system.

The new landscape can be of different natures, defined by playfulness or relaxation, or simply by the landscape, such as a forest or a pine forest. The houses in the cluster will be directed towards the landscape, and the internal space will be liminal and respectful to avoid excessively invading privacy or replicating an intensive system. The advantage of this settlement system is linked to the size of the intervention, which allows for discussions over even a large area without losing the cluster's scale factor and completely isolating oneself from the landscape. The collective dimension of the campsite, understood as optional in comparison to the private one, can thus consistently be replicated in relation to the natural element of reference. Furthermore, landscape construction in concentrated areas has significant ecological value. For example, the concentration of tree elements reduces thermal impact and carbon dioxide production. Developing a technical landscape at the service of clusters is also possible, for example, by working with water as a mitigation or cleaning system that reacts to houses.

Finally, with a view to the transition of the campsite sector, and therefore taking into account the long term of the accommodation facility, i.e. the replacement of mobile homes, this settlement system can determine a place's identity construction. The landscape created for the installation of the cluster, being independent, can become a place of reference, a stable element around which to replace the housing compartments. While becoming mandatory for the installation of houses, the ecological value of this strategy must be taken into consideration due to its double relationship with time and, therefore, with the use of space: the time of the holiday, which is repeated over the years, and the time of the houses that change in relation to a new fixed landscape.

DIRECTED SYSTEM

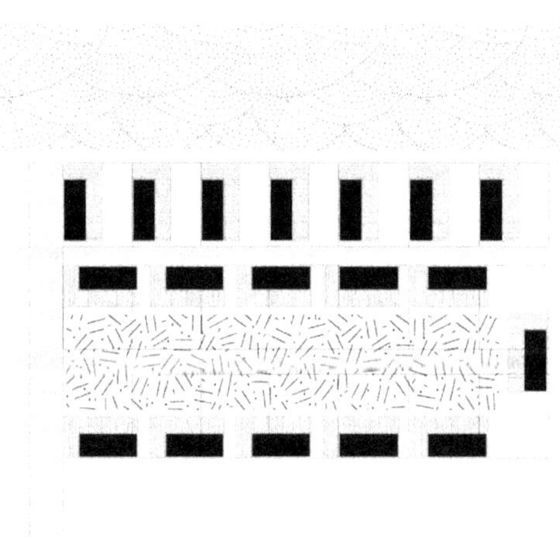

THE UNITS CAN BE ORGANIZED TO DEFINE A NEW MAIN LANDSCAPE.ÙMAINTAINGIN THE FIRST LINE TO GET THE BEST VIEW, THE OTHER PART OF THE CAMPSITE DESCRIBES A NEW LANDSCAPE.
THE UNITS ARE SETTLED AROUND AN AMPLE SPACE THAT CAN BE DEVELOPED AS A COPY OF THE PREVALENT ONE OR AS A DIFFERENT NATURAL SYSTEM.
THE DIMENSION OF THIS SPACE ALLOWS HAVING HERE SERVICES AND LÒISIRS DIRECTED TO THE FAMILY OF THE UNITS.

Figure 2.13 Directed System

ACT 6: MEDIUM TIME

The construction of the city of tourism, linked to the experience of outdoor holidays, involves a reflection on the landscape and the scale of the intervention. The dual-timing characteristic of this type of settlement generates reflections on the landscape that must go in a virtuous direction; one of maintenance and enhancement. The environmental impact of the campsite, mainly linked to the phenomenon of overtourism, must be compensated for with the correct planning of the space and strategic management of the service.

Finally, the image of the landscape, depicted with respect to the prevailing landscape, must not expire in a thematised replica, but be based on a thorough understanding of the local habitat. In this critical context, mobile homes distort the perception of the landscape towards a neo-vernacular housing dimension. However, the theme of the village must not be defined in a linguistic/formal way, but rather as a spatial reference. Settlement fragmentation based on the clustering system, combined with landscape construction that contains natural and non-natural elements, allows for a more direct perception of the context, even over extensive areas.

Furthermore, the fragmented management of the landscape allows the enhancement of areas of the campsite, even those far from the prevailing landscape. This enhancement is not only functional to the service, but also insists on the quality of the open space and, therefore, of the landscape of the open-air accommodation facility. Read as the matrix of the artificial/natural landscape, open-air accommodation facilities can therefore be an unprecedented laboratory to apply urban strategies linked to sustainability and nature. In fragile contexts where the urban sector is weakened, such as the outer fringes of the intermittent city of tourism, the campsite can become a place to enhance the natural image of the place. The housing system of the mobile home gives rise to settlement suggestions, such as those discussed, which can inspire any new settlements with similar characteristics.

An unusual field of application will be dealt with in the next chapter, namely that of refugee camps. Even in these contexts, where the measurement of time does not coincide with the perception of the urban sector, the need to construct the landscape is contingent. The landscape of the refugee camps is defined in a functionalistic way because it is calibrated on the immediacy inherent in the constitution of the refugee camp. However, experience has shown that the timings of this housing system go beyond immediacy and even those of the city of tourism, so much so that they are considered, within this research, as examples of a long time of living in relation to the temporariness of the city.

Notes

1 The Italian Tourism Code (Annex 1 of Legislative Decree 79/2011).
2 Italian legislation limits the possibility of constructing total cubic meters of buildings according to the territorial extension and the categorisation of the territory.
3 Costa Smeralda is the name of a portion of the territory of the Sardinia region in Italy, and the subject of urban and architectural planning in the 1950s commissioned by Aga Khan and directed mainly by the architect Louis Vietti.
4 For this in-depth analysis, refer to the proceedings of the Xxix Conference Of The International Seminar On Urban Form 2022 Łódź – Kraków | September 6–11, 2022 Urban Redevelopment and Revitalization A Multidisciplinary Perspective – The city of entertainment as an experimentation field for improving the daily public space by Margherita Capotorto and Luca Trabattoni.
5 Henry David Thoreau, *Walden or life in woods*.
6 Robert Burton, author of *The Anatomy of Melancholy*, 1621.
7 The Corbin quote is found in the text by Ana Swanson, author of "The weird origins of going to the beach", 2016.
8 The name refers to the Enlightenment movement.
9 "Tourism, the act and process of spending time away from home in pursuit of recreation, relaxation and pleasure, while making use of the commercial provision of services. As such, tourism is a product of modern social arrangements, beginning in western Europe in the 17th century, although it has antecedents in Classical antiquity" (Walton, J.K. "tourism". *Encyclopedia Britannica*, 14 March 2023. Available at: https://www.britannica.com/topic/tourism).
10 The idea of offering excursions to the working class came to Cook as he "walked from Market Harborough to Leicester to attend a meeting of the Temperance Society". With the opening of the extended Midland Counties Railway, he planned to take a group of temperance activists from Leicester station to a teetotal rally in Loughborough, 11 miles away. On 5 July 1841 Thomas Cook accompanied some 500 people, who paid one shilling each for the return journey by train, on his first excursion. During the following three summers he planned and conducted outings for local temperance societies and Sunday school children (Robert Ingle, *Thomas Cook of Leicester*, Burford, Headstart History, 1991.

11 Thomas Hiram Holding was the author of *Cycle and Camp* and the *Camper's Handbook* and founder of the Association of Cyclists, now called the Campsite and Caravanning Club.

12 Terence Young, "The religious roots of America's love for camping, how a minister's accidental bestseller launched the country's first outdoor craze", *Zocalo Public Square*, 2018a, Available at https://www.zocalopublicsquare.org/.

13 A unique model made by Jules Secretat for the engineer Henri Lafitte in 1903. Jules Secretat would have used it to visit his region between the Loire and the Pyrenees and would have exhibited it at the finish line of the famous Paris–Madrid, which stopped in Bordeaux.

14 Terence Young, "A Brief History of the RV", *Smithsonian*, 2018b, https://www.smithsonianmag.com/innovation/brief-history-rv-180970195/.

15 The Act designated four bank holidays in England, Wales and Ireland (Easter Monday; Whit Monday; the first Monday in August; and 26 December if it fell on a weekday) and five in Scotland (New Year's Day, or the next day if it fell on a Sunday; Good Friday; the first Monday in May; the first Monday in August; and Christmas Day, or the next day if it fell on a Sunday).

16 Center for Social Studies, Documentation, Information and Action and Central Office of Charities and Social Services, "French Information", Social life: cahiers du CEDIAS, July 1966, pp. 333–334 (read online, available at https://gallica.bnf.fr/ark:/12148/bpt6k6315096n/f19, accessed 9 March 2022).

17 In fact, article 36 of the labor charter reads: "The worker has the right to a remuneration proportionate to the quantity and quality of his work and in any case sufficient to ensure a free and dignified existence for himself and his family. The maximum length of the working day is established by law. The worker has the right to weekly rest and paid annual holidays, and cannot renounce them".

18 The Magic Villages were founded by publisher Paul Morihien, painter Jean Cocteau and sports journalist Dimitri Philippoff. The idea was to create a vacation spot for his sports friends, and more generally for sports and outdoor activities enthusiasts (https://www.clubmed.it/).

19 The "Calvi Olympic Club", was founded again by Dimitri Philippoff. The club is located on a beach three or four kilometers from the port, on land owned by the family of Edith Fillipachi, who manages the course. Advertising posters praise a "French-British canvas village, with English comfort, French cuisine with a full two-week stay, American bar, dance floor, international atmosphere" and "Horizon club in Calvi" referring to the "French-British Village", domiciled at 8 rue Boudreau in Paris. The village is home to around 120 people, mostly French but also English, who share tents, meals together, a volleyball court, a bar, dance floor and

water cows hung from trees to wash. The buffet formula is already present, with grilled food and wine at your discretion, as well as one gala evening a week. Some 70 years later, the Calvi Olympic club still has 250 cabins, 108 of which have shared toilets. The tents have been replaced by bungalows equipped with kitchens and toilets (https://www.clubmed.it/).

20 Originally frequented by singles and young couples, Club Med later became a holiday destination for families, with the first Mini Club inaugurated in 1967 in Donoratico (LI). In 1974 Club Med's finances collapsed due to various negative factors, due to which Trigano had to resort to a heavy capital increase. At that point new shareholders came into play, including Gianni Agnelli, who brought money into the club's coffers and facilitated the opening of villages in Italy. Through the IFIL holding, he retained 23.9% of the capital until 2004. In the 1990s, Club Med went through a phase of decline due to strong competition. In 1995 it ceased to exist as a club in the legal sense, becoming a company in its own right. Two years earlier, Serge Trigano took over from his father, but in 1997 he was replaced by Philippe Bourguignon, former president of Euro Disney S.C.A. Bourguignon wanted to transform Club Med from a holiday village company to a service company. A chain of gyms, bar-restaurant complexes called Club Med World in Paris and Montréal and a type of resort designed for young adults, Oyyo, were launched, with the first of these opening in Monastir, Tunisia. The Jet Tours travel agency was also created (https://www.clubmed.it/).

21 The problem being corsair raids that pushed the inhabitants to live in the hinterland instead of the coasts.

22 Extract from the introduction to point 6 of the Building Regulations of the Costa Smeralda Consortium - External arrangements and Gardens.

23 Various authors, "Italian life", vol. 24, Rome, Presidency of the Council of Ministers, Information Service, p. 939. Accessed on 19 February 2020.

24 Archive of the Italian Touring club, Available at https://www.digitouring.it/, Accessed on 9 March 2023.

25 Ibid.

26 Italian entrepreneur and philanthropist, founder of the men's luxury clothing company Ermenegildo Zegna.

27 Italian architect and designer active in the 1950s. Two-time winner of the Compasso d'Oro.

28 Compasso d'Oro is one of the most authoritative awards related to industrial design.

29 Pirelli, information and technical magazine. Available at http://search.fondazionepirelli.org/bookreader/riviste/RivistaPirelli/1968_9.html?q=&start=79&lang=it&fbclid=IwAR21Job517xv501CswiFoLVBiq8Ax6Q5CZr9ifLRN7x-_UUbK_5uRL – wxxw, Accessed on 9 March 2022.

30 It should be noted that joining was not an exclusive procedure but could also be done upon arrival at the villages.

31 Architectural neorealism is an architectural current of post-War Italian rationalism. The trend can be identified as the first reaction to the Modern movement in architecture, which developed in Italy, and is linked to the broader cultural movement precisely defined Neorealism, which had its development in the years immediately following the end of the Second World War.

32 The two projects are presented and described in the magazine *Architettura, cronache e storia* (1970), 175, with a preface by Carlo Aymonino and a dialogue between the designers. The village of Ostuni is located in the province of Brindisi, in Puglia. With an accommodation capacity of around 600 beds, it is structured in traditional hotel rooms, studio-type rooms and private accommodation. The restaurant and reception services are located in the center of the village and form the hub of the complex. The Valtur village of Isola Capo Rizzuto overlooks the Ionian Sea, 20km south of Crotone. It is surrounded by 100-hectares of centuries-old olive grove. The functions present in the Calabrian village are the same as those of Ostuni: a central nucleus with restaurants, bars and commercial and reception services, and accommodation grouped into three areas.

33 The Metabolosta movement, or Metabolist group, is a group of Japanese architects, including Kisho Kurokawa, Kikutake and others, who were partly influenced by the figure of Kenzo Tange, and partly for personal reasons, produced some urban visions that became famous in the 1950s and 1960s. They were related to the theme of artificial soil, megestratuura and capsules as a minimal housing system.

34 Office established at the end of the 18th century in France for the management and maintenance of roads. See the essay by Marc Desportes, *Landscapes in motion. Transport and perception of space between the 18th and 20th centuries,* Milano, Libri Scheiwiller, illustrated edition, 2008.

35 Among the studies that analyse the origin, diffusion and history of Tuscan coastal pine forests, see the 1993 work by Antonio Gabrielli "Origin of coastal pine forests in Tuscany".

36 https://www.beniculturalionline.it/post.php?n=1522.

37 https://www.ioamoiviaggi.it/vacanza-in-toscana-nella-pineta-di-roccamare/.

38 Francesco Ginanni (Ravenna, December 13, 1716–Ravenna, March 8, 1766) was an Italian naturalist, biologist and botanist, author of: *Istoria civile e naturale delle pinete ravennati*, Roma, Giovanni Generoso Salomoni, 1774.

39 Stefano Grassi, Full Professor of Institutions of Public Law at the Department of Legal Sciences of the University of Florence.

40 The same article was integrated in 2021 by introducing the concepts of biodiversity and ecosystems – Protect the environment, biodiversity and ecosystems, also in the interest of future generations. State law regulates the methods and forms of animal protection. Article 9 Italian constitution 2021.
41 Weimar Costitution (11 August 1919).
42 Gilles Clément (Argenton-sur-Creuse, October 6, 1943) is a French agronomist, biologist, writer, entomologist, landscape designer and teacher at the École nationale du paysage in Versailles. He is among the best known and most influential landscape designers in Europe, and is the theorist of planetary garden, the moving garden and the concept of the third landscape. He has many essays and novels to his credit.
43 Adrian Geuze (Dordrecht, 28 October 1960, Prof., Ir., RLA, OALA, Principal in Charge, project director, Landscape Architect). In 1987 Adriaan Geuze was one of the founders of West 8 urban design & landscape architecture b.v., a leading urban design practice in Europe.
44 Matthew Skjonsberg is director of Praxis Institute and lecturer on New Civic Landscapes and Public Health (ETHZ) and Did You Say Park? (EPFL). He is of the first generation in his family not to farm, and emulates that practice by working for self-representation towards self-determination with indigenous communities through civic design
45 Maurice Merleau-Ponty (Rochefort-sur-Mer, March 14, 1908–Paris, May 3, 1961) was a French philosopher, a leading exponent of 20th-century French phenomenology.
46 William John Thomas Mitchell (born March 24, 1942) is an American academic. Mitchell is the Gaylord Donnelley Distinguished Service Professor of English and Art History at the University of Chicago. He is also the editor of *Critical Inquiry*, and contributes to the journal *October*.
47 Rosa Barba i Casanovas (1948–2000) was an architect, urbanist and landscape theorist, and the planner that introduced the contemporary landscape design culture in Spain. She founded the first Landscape Architecture Degree in Barcelona, and the Landscape Architecture Biennial that awards the prize to Landscape Architecture Projects that have her name.
48 UNESCO (2005) Operational Guidelines for the Implementation of the World Heritage Convention Archived copy, at whc.unesco.org. URL consulted on 5 October 2023 (archived from the original URL on 24 July 2008). UNESCO World Heritage Centre. Paris. Page 83.
49 **Codice del turismo** - Allegato al Decreto legislativo 23.05.2011 n° 79 - Gazz. Uff. 6 giugno 2011, n. 129
50 **Codice del turismo** - Allegato al Decreto legislativo 23.05.2011 n° 79 - Gazz. Uff. 6 giugno 2011, n. 129- art 13
51 Ibid
52 Regulation 7 August 2018, n. 47/R – Implementation regulation of the regional law 20 December 2016 n. 86 (Consolidated text of the regional tourism system) – Official Bulletin n. 36, part one, of 10 August 2018.

53 Device of the art. 142 Code of cultural heritage and landscape Code of cultural heritage and landscape, THIRD PART – Landscape assets, Title I – Protection and enhancement, Chapter II – Identification of landscape assets.

54 Outdoor Report Estate 2021 Previsioni Italia – Human Company and Thrends, p. 44.

55 https://www.britannica.com/place/Field-of-Cloth-of-Gold.

56 "The requirements for campsite sites are laid down in the states' Campsite and Weekend Parks Regulations. Campsite sites generally need to have an access road from a public road, with access control (barrier), reception and assignment of places, an area for waiting vehicles, visitor's car parks and internal access with roads adequate for fire service vehicles (width~ min. 3.0 m).

Campsite sites and motorhome parks should be separated. A place should be provided for each caravan or motorhome. These places are min. 75 m^2 (65 m^2 if car parking spaces are provided separately) and are grouped into sections of 20 places by fire roads m wide). It may be necessary to provide firebreak strips next to the boundaries.

Campsite sites have the following communal facilities: drinking water taps (one tap for every 20 places supplied from the public water main), electricity sockets (parking places for motorhomes and larger caravans should ideally have water supply, drains and electricity supply), fire hydrants and fire extinguishers (one fire extinguisher per 40 places) sanitary facilities with: toilet blocks (guideline: 1 block per 100 places with: 4 WCs/2 urinals/1 washbasin (gents'), 6 WC/ 1 washbasin (ladies'), 1 we for the disabled), washing facilities (guideline for each 100 places: 3 showers, 5 washbasins for gents and ladies, 1 shower and washroom for the disabled), sink for washing crockery and clothes, emptying facility for waste water and toilets, sufficient and appropriately distributed waste bins – telephone line with emergency call function, kiosk, supermarket, snack bar or restaurant, leisure facilities (play area, sports grounds, barbecue site, open area)" (Neufert and Neufert, 2012, p. 187).

57 Xxix Conference Of The International Seminar On Urban Form 2022 Łódź – Kraków | September 6–11, 2022 *Urban Redevelopment and Revitalisation A Multidisciplinary Perspective* – The city of entertainment as an experimentation field for improving the daily public space by Margherita Capotorto and Luca Trabattoni.

58 For the Italian regulation, a buffer zone is an area of territory within which special constraints exist in order to protect the object of the constraint. This object can be naturalistic, artistic or infrastructural. The need for respect can be both to protect the object of the restriction and to avoid dangerous situations for citizens.

3 Epilogue

The Experience of Refugee Camps as Long Temporary Settlements (Long Time)

The last "timing" this treatment is compared to is that of the refugee camps. The theme of the refugee camp may seem extremely distant from that of camping, and in part, it is. However, without considering the functional distance, and instead considering the shape of the settlement, the two examples appear more comparable.

With respect to the refugee camp, it is difficult to define an absolute time limit, given that every emergency evolves over time. All the camps, however, live in a condition of permanent temporariness until they are dismantled. However, unfortunately, experience shows us that in the last 70 years, this has happened very rarely. As Manuel Herz explains in his research, refugee camps began to be used worldwide in the early twentieth century (Herz, 2012. However, if any of those built from the beginning of the twentieth century up to the end of the Second World War had a definite conclusion over time, after the Second World War, the dismantling of the camp became an extraordinary and sporadic event, so much so that today, the longest-lived refugee camps are up to 70 years old. Significant changes, such as the number of camp inhabitants or the host country's conditions, inevitably accompany such a duration.

For this reason, the time spent in the refugee camps is defined as "long" in this discussion because it far exceeds the time spent in any other "temporary city" seen up to now. It is a paradoxical time, complicated to plan and to judge. What is certain is that the inconsistency between the presumed temporariness of the settlement and its actual temporality is at the basis of many of the hardships that characterise the refugee camps.

DOI: 10.4324/9781003468530-4

According to Michel Agier, two problems related to the refugee camp make it a paradoxical habitat:

> The permanent precariousness and the status of the space… the self-evident fact of its extraterritoriality… As a consequence of these conditions, "within this 'extra-territorial' space, the exceptional situation that the refugees encounter becomes the ordinary texture of their existence".
>
> (Agier, 2011 p. 71)

Numerous experts have expressed their views on this issue, proposing a rethinking of the refugee camp, no longer only as an emergency, but as an actual urban settlement.

This last chapter deals with the theme of the "refugee camp", starting from the following assumption: if the refugee camp is to be read as a city, its construction must go beyond emergency pragmatism by thinking of the space of people for people. In the face of this reflection, can the conclusions relating to open-air accommodation facilities be helpful for a rethinking of the settlement system?

The time of the refugee camps is contradictory. *Refugee camps* are settlements that arise to respond to an extraordinary situation. The aspect to this of emergency and necessity involves a pragmatic construction of space. The extra-ordinariness of the emergency is characterised by a limited, albeit undefined, temporality. In this indeterminacy lies the paradox of the refugee camp. This aspect must be defined by its three fundamental components: temporal, identity and the urban form.

Temporally, the "refugee camp" experiences an overt dissociation between its programmatic nature and its effectiveness: the assumed emergency timing is indefinable and, therefore, cannot be evaluated in terms of coincidence with the effective duration of the refugee camp itself, which, therefore, will always be inadequate.

From an identity point of view, understood as a sense of belonging to a place, as a sense of community, the status of "refugee" as defined by UNHCR imposes a dissociation. As Agier suggests, a shared sense of not belonging unites the camp's guests. The camps are born as host structures, and refugees can maintain their status, and therefore their rights, only within the camp's perimeter. This constrictive condition determines a dual relationship with the structure: salvific and, at the same time, coercive.

Finally, a third aspect characterises the refugee camp linked to its physical form. These places are built on a fixed dimensional basis, but leave the participatory space to the residents (to the extent of the construction of the housing unit). The dimensions provided by and organisation by UNHCR are decisive for the "military camp" shape of the camp itself; however, contrary to this, the shape of the inhabited spaces is left to the refugees, who can use the material provided by UNHCR. The result is a hybrid image of the refugee camp, which in part recalls the slums of large cities and in part reminds one of traditional villages, codified on the aggregation of simple housing forms. The UNHCR requirements need to include the study of interstitial and relational spaces, which are instead decisive in the realities of villages, as has been demonstrated for the spontaneous Saharawi camps (Herz, 2012. This hybrid status also establishes an unresolved situation from a spatial point of view, and therefore a situation inadequate to the needs of those who live in the camp, who live in an emergency that aspires to be an urban context.

The theme of refugees, and the aspirations and constraints related to their permanence in the camp has been the object of anthropological and sociological studies and research, which remain a fundamental cultural background for this research. However, the final theme of this chapter will be the theme of urban form concerning non-residential spatialities. It is only possible to approach such a complex issue by considering the critical debate between the refugee camp and the emergent premises that determine its origin. Before addressing the issue of urban form, the definitions and organisation of UNHCR will be shown. We will then go on to illustrate the extent of the number of people involved in the refugee camps and how these people, despite the temporary and emergency of the camp, in some cases, organise themselves permanently by seeking a community dimension. The critical debate regarding refugee camps is oriented towards the urban potential of these contexts, not from a morphological point of view but from a sociological point of view. The "long" time spent in the refugee camps calls for attention to the potential of the communities present, intending to improve the quality of life for refugees.

Finally, we will focus on the issue of urban form to illustrate how the comparison with accommodation facilities for open-air tourism can be constructive even in these emergencies. In both cases, as we will see, the element that determines the form that we perceive of the settlement is that of the housing unit. In both cases, the time factor determines the urban form of the temporary city.

Definition and Organisation

First, clarifying the context of what a refugee camp is, and who is involved, is essential. Although similar in primary conditions, not all refugee camps are monitored and planned a priori.

> Nobody knows how many refugee camps there are in the world. In 2012, 700 were officially surveyed, but hundreds of others escaped the count: small camps organised by communities and local administrations; temporary camps created by the security authorities; small religious camps; informal camps established with the gradual assembly of fleeing refugees; also, families host hundreds of thousands of refugees in their own homes or live in squats in cities[1].

For this reason, the object of study in this chapter will be precisely that of the refugee camps designed and managed by UNHCR, the section of the United Nations explicitly dedicated to refugees. Some exclusions should be specified: refugee camps within European territory, which have lived and continue to live a different and, at times, more complicated experience, will not be considered; and the camps within occupied Palestinian territories will also not be considered.

The European situations, as can be seen by reading the UNHCR[2] reports (such as that on the famous Jungle of Calais or the Moira Camp of Lesbos), represent or have represented complicated housing conditions, whose dynamics differ when compared with those in Africa or Asia and therefore will not be investigated in this text.

The refugee camps inside occupied Palestinian territories are instead managed and built by UNRWA[3], the section of the United Nations specifically for Palestinian refugees. UNRWA was founded in 1948 following the Arab–Israeli conflict[4]. The work of UNRWA concerns a socially complicated emergency condition, and the refugee camps must be read as part of the debate on the complicated Palestinian question. For this reason, these settlements will not be considered as part of the subject of this book either.

Instead, the characteristics of the refugee camps designed by UNHCR outside Europe will be illustrated, mainly those in the African continent, which have common characteristics with respect to the context in which they are located, the climate and the human situations they host. These refugee camps refer to the emergency manual written by UNHCR and therefore have standard, shared features that can also be recognised from a morphological point of view. The evolution of these refugee camps over time intervenes in this original structure, with additions and modifications that are not substantial but evident due to the autonomous actions of the refugees.

UNHCR has defined precisely what a refugee camp is and how it is made. The emergency handbook, published in 1982, is a digital guide containing information for setting up a camp. At the very beginning of the paper, one can find some key points:

1 – UNHCR discourages the establishment of formal settlements and (whenever possible) prefers alternatives to camps, provided they effectively protect and assist people of concern.
2 – Shelter should be adapted according to the geographical context, climate, cultural practice and habits, local availability of skills, and accessibility to adequate construction materials in any given country.
3 – Due consideration should be given to the operational phase. What may be deemed adequate during an emergency in terms of shelter (for example, plastic sheeting, tents) and average camp area per person cannot be regarded as adequate in a protracted displacement situation[5].

There is, therefore, as a starting point, the awareness of the inadequacy of the settlement in relation to "traditional" living. This assumption must be taken into account when considering the definition of standards made by UNHCR. The warning about time remains suspended, but the indefiniteness of the continuation indicated in the guide finds neither a temporal specification nor a compositional reactivity.

According to UNHCR, from a technical point of view, a refugee camp is defined as a temporary living space designed to house people in difficulty who have been displaced from their national territory.

> Refugee camps are temporary facilities built to provide immediate assistance and protection to people who have been forced to flee their homes due to violence, conflict or persecution. Refugee

camps are initially designed as a short-term solution to keep people safe during specific emergencies, but emergency situations can become protracted, resulting in people living in camps for years or even decades[6].

In defining a camp, the choice of site is essential. The evaluation points of the site must include topographic evaluations, the presence of water resources and infrastructures that guarantee accessibility[7]. All of this says little about the quality of the refugee camp being built and managed; it is a pragmatic and generalised approach linked to the need to define a model and standards that can be adapted to every situation.

Refugee camps are found almost all over the world, from Europe to Asia to Africa. Regardless of geographic location, UNHCR applies the same dimensional standards:

Indicator: Average Camp Area Per Person (m^2)

Standard	*Acceptable Range*	*Unacceptable Range*	*Critical Range*
45	35	34–30	29

Considering the standard dimension as the usual one, it must follow that $30m^2$ per person will be necessary for roads, footpaths, educational facilities, sanitation, security, firebreaks, administration, water storage, distribution points, markets, storage of relief items and shelter plots. This excludes, however, any land needed for significant agricultural activities or livestock. The remaining 15 m^2 per person is allocated to household gardens attached to the family plot, which should be included in the site plan from the outset.

This sizing, which incorporates the standards indicated by SPHERE[8], is the starting point for giving generic settlement indications (distance between buildings, minimum height, fire safety, minimum equipment), which is defined according to the family unit. The family is understood as a unit of 4/6 people, and becomes the mathematical matrix that determines the size of the refugee camp:

Module	*Context*	*Approx. No. of People*
Family	1 family	4–6 people
1 community	16 families	80 people

Module	*Context*	*Approx. No. of People*
1 block	16 communities	1,250 people
1 sector	4 blocks	5,000 people
1 camp	4 sectors	20,000 people

The result is an organised modular system, which is rationalised planimetrically and defines an orthogonal grid. Sizing according to the services follows, in this case, in a mathematical way, for which reference is made to the manual.

We want to underline how the pragmatic approach of necessity does not give qualitative indications. Although this concern is present in the manual, which states that "the plan should take into account the social organisation of refugees and the principles of planning of the individual modules" (UNHCR, 2007, p. 215), it does not explicitly state how the plan of the camp should react to the situation of the refugees' society.

Another interesting matter to underline in the manual concerns urban planning. The manual states that modular planning does not necessarily mean using a rigid layout for the site. In fact, the rigid layout should be avoided in every way possible because it disrupts community interaction (UNHCR, 2007, p. 216). However, the applied settlement system clearly shows its rigidity, which is reminiscent of military or prison, rather than residential, references. This settlement structure becomes evident if we look at some relatively young refugee camps. For example, some Ethiopian refugee camps in the Tigray region (2008), clearly show this plan. Until 2018, four

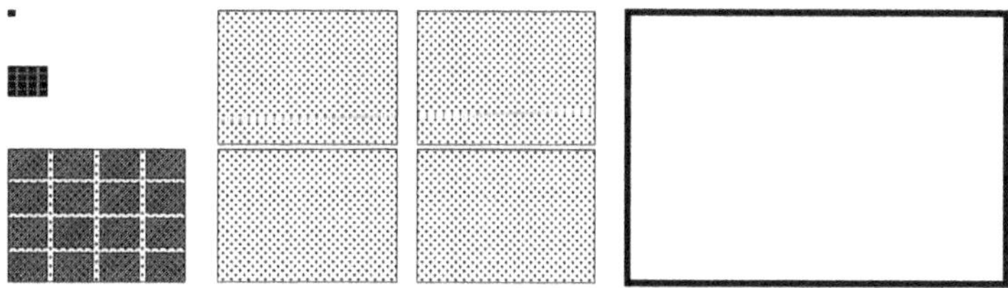

Figure 3.1 Refugee Camp Diagrams

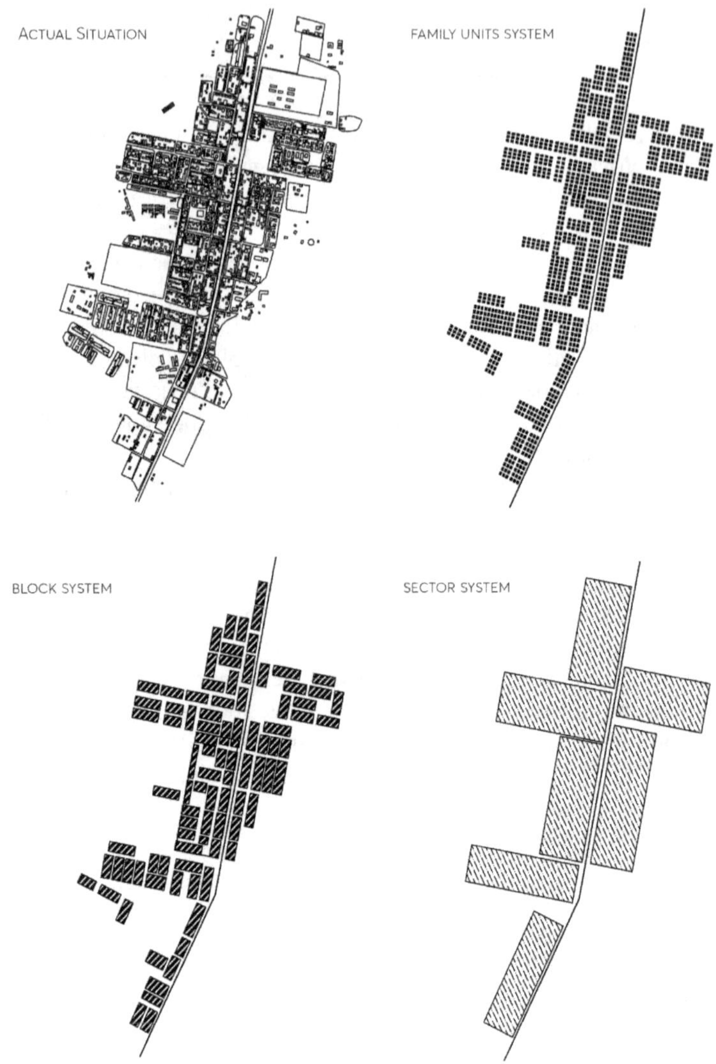

Figure 3.2 Mai-Aini Refugee Camp

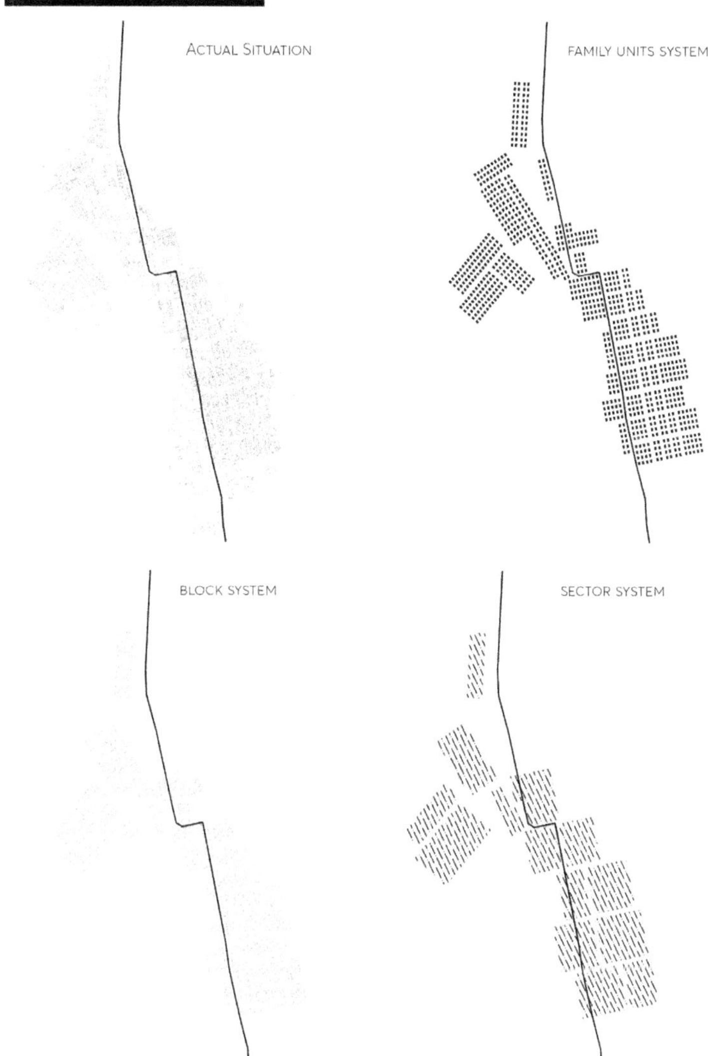

Figure 3.3 Adi-Harush Refugee Camp

refugee camps were present in this same region, more or less similar and of the same size. However, due to the civil war involving Tigray, as of today, two of the four refugee camps have been destroyed or evacuated. Nevertheless, these two remaining refugee camps remain active and close to each other. The first, the Mai-Aini refugee camp, was established in May 2008 to accommodate Eritrean refugees seeking international protection. In 2018 there were 17,825 refugees registered inside the camp. The second, the Adi-Harush refugee camp, was established in March 2010 to accommodate Eritrean refugees seeking international protection. In 2018 there were 10,599 refugees registered inside the camp.

Who Lives in the Refugee Camp?

Anyone who lives in or is hosted by the refugee camp is defined as a refugee (Prima Facie Refugee). As is possible to read in the Glossary of the UNHCR Global Report 2005,

> persons recognised as refugees, by a State or UNHCR based on objective criteria related to the circumstances in their country of origin that justify a presumption that they meet the criteria of the applicable refugee definition. See also "Group-based protection responses"[9].

It is necessary to have a clear vision of the number, in terms of people living in refugee camps, to understand the importance of studying these places. In the world, there are currently 79.5 million people who have been forced to leave their homes to flee wars, persecution and severe conditions of insecurity. According to the latest report published on 18 June by the United Nations High Commissioner for Refugees (UNHCR), this accounts for 1% of the world's population. Among them, approximately 22% of the world's refugee population lives in refugee camps – an estimated 6.6 million people. Out of them, 4.5 million reside in planned and managed camps, and approximately 2 million are sheltered in self-settled camps (UNHCR Global Trends, 2020.

In the last decade, about 100 million people have been displaced from their country of origin, and of these, only 3.9 million have returned to their country of origin. At the same time, 754.5 million have obtained new citizenship. Moreover, the proportion of the world's population that has been displaced has continued to grow. 1% of the world's population, or 1 in 97 people, is now forcibly displaced.[10] Climate change and natural disasters can exacerbate threats forcing people to flee within their own countries or across international borders. The interaction between climate, conflict, hunger, poverty and persecution creates ever more complex emergencies (UNHCR Global Trends, 2020 pp. 8–12).

The extension of the refugee camp phenomenon and the temporal inconsistencies lead to a reflection on the nature of the refugee camp beyond its technical definition. The debate on whether to recognise the refugee camp as a real city or not is at the centre of the critical debate.

Talking about "refugee camps" is perhaps generic, and it is, therefore, essential to understanding the reason for the debate mentioned above that we are aware of the size of the settlements we are talking about through some specific examples:

- The Dadaab refugee camp in Kenya, for example, is considered one of the settlements with the largest number of refugees in the world: the settlement consists of three camps, and the 2020 update had 218,873 refugees.

  There are three camps: Dagahaley, Ifo and Hagadera sited in the Lagdera (Dadaab) district, and in the neighbouring Fafi district. Dadaab is home to a population that arrived in the 90s and is now in the third generation. As is possible to read on the UNHCR official site:

  > The camps resemble naturally-grown towns and have developed into commercial hubs connecting north-eastern Kenya and southern Somalia. During the Horn of Africa famine in 2011, two camps, Ifo 2 and Kambioos, were established to cater for the influx. These two camps have, however, been closed with the reduction of the numbers in Dadaab due to the voluntary return programme[11].

- The Zaatari camp, in Jordan, was founded on 28 July in 2012 in order to host Syrians fleeing the violence in the ongoing Syrian War that erupted in March 2011; today, it contains 82,268 refugees. The numbers of Zataari clarify the situation:

> The Tents have been replaced by 25,000 prefabricated shelters; over 20,000 births were recorded in 2022, It exists a bustling market features 1,800 shops; it exists eight medical facilities provide free health care; more than 30 organisations operating in the camp; and that Zaatari camp is powered by solar energy; and among all these data, only 4 per cent of refugees hold work permits.
>
> (Carlisle, 2022) [12]

In addition to specific insights, a simple panel can give an idea about the dimensions and timing of some of the biggest camps in the world (UNHCR, 2022):

Camp Name	*Location*	*Foundation Year*	*Population*
Kutupalong	Bangladesh	1991	598,195
Kakuma	Kenya	1992	248,929
Dadaab refugee complex	Kenya	1992	233,661
Zaatari	Jordan	2012	77,781
Mai Aini	Ethiopia	2008	11,718 (as of 2018)
Cooper's Camp	West Bengal	1947	7,000

Refugees' low quality of life is one of the significant problems associated with living in refugee camps.

The refugee camp was born of the need for containing isolation with internal and specific laws, and the inhabitants of the camp, therefore, remain the inhabitants of the "outside", "an excess of humanity outside the walls" (Rahola, 2003, p. 104). The social extraneousness of the camp's inhabitants is determined by the very nature of the camp as well as by the causes of its foundation. Inside the camp, the refugee does not have to work, but lives as a supporter linked to the camp. However, the rights of "*refugee*" (health, education, maintenance) are linked to permanence within the space of the camp, outside of which one is not allowed to go. The camp, therefore, becomes something one cannot leave.

If refugee camps respond to the loss of certain forms of belonging, they generate a form of involuntary belonging, recognised as "unpleasant" and, therefore, limited over time. Refugees are primarily stateless, then fleeing their country of origin. From a legislative point of view, the refugee camp is an independent place from the host country, so those who live in the camp do not live in the host country. The refugee camp thus becomes a sort of "non-place" sui generis, a space "outside" as defined by Rahola (Rahola, 2003) resolved with the temporal variable.

The UNHCR has recognised the inadequacy of the situation in the refugee camp by pursuing policies related to what are defined as "Durable Solutions" as opposed to those in the refugee camp. *The Handbook for Planning and Implementing Development Assistance Programs for Refugees* (DAR, 2005) is based on the implementation of three key strategies: "Repatriation; local integration; Resettlements" (UNHCR, 2003 p. 11). These strategies have also been reaffirmed by the 4Rs Framework program: *Repatriation, Reintegration, Rehabilitation and Reconstruction.* In both these cases, in addition to the admission by UNHCR that it cannot act alone, it appears clear that the strategic approach is overcoming the "refugee camp" as a definitive place.

However, some experiences start from the refugee camp as a place to live. *The Kakuma refugee camp* is located in the Northwestern region of Kenya, one of the biggest camps in the world[13]. The camp was established in 1992 following the arrival of the "Lost Boys of Sudan". During that year, large groups of Ethiopian refugees fled their country following the fall of the Ethiopian government. Somalia had also experienced high insecurity and civil strife, causing people to flee. With an influx of new arrivals in 2014, Kakuma surpassed its capacity by over 58,000 individuals, leading to congestion in various sections. Following negotiations between UNHCR, the National Government, the County Government of Turkana and the host community, land for a new settlement was identified in Kalobeyei, 20km from Kakuma town[14].

Kalobey represents an exciting example of trying to overcome the paradoxes of the refugee camp by transforming the settlement into an established situation.

> The Kalobeyei Integrated Socio-Economic Development Plan (KISEDP) was initially devised to support a new approach aimed at establishing a settlement in a place called Kalobeyei in Turkana West, where both refugees and host populations would live together rather than a separate refugee camp.
>
> (UNHCR, 2018, p. III)

The plan proposed by UNHCR is interesting because it plans a long-term integration process between the local community and the refugees in the camp by generating a hybrid housing context. The project started in 2015 and is aimed to be completed in 2030. The phases in which the project is organised foresee a development over time involving an ever-greater involvement between the camp's population and the host population, both from an economic and social point of view.

> The new approach was developed around the "Choice Theory" to allow refugees and the host population to maximise their potential in an enabling environment. The theory has two main building blocks which inform the overall goal of KISEDP. Firstly, it aims to create an enabling environment in which inclusive service delivery and local capacities are strengthened, legal frameworks and policies are improved, a conducive environment for investment and job creation is promoted, and communities' resilience is strengthened. It also aims to build people's skills and capabilities to function successfully in this new environment and to enhance the overall local economy.
>
> (UNHCR, 2018, p. 5)

Another exciting example is the one proposed by the same association for the *Nakivale camp.*

> Established in 1958, Nakivale Refugee Settlement is one of the oldest refugee camps in the world. However, it is also filled with surprises, innovation, beauty, and determination around every corner. Nakivale—and the people who live there—prove that a refugee camp does not automatically equal scarcity and tragedy. Instead, it can be filled with hope, community, and abundance[15].

In the presentation of Alike, some activities related to the refugee camp are explained: Opporotunigee is a hub that helps the refugee in personal and professional growth; and then there are activities like yoga classes, music studio, art classes, acrobats and others. These social strategies demonstrate an idea about the camp that exceeds the temporariness and manages the refugee camp as a "real" urban settlement. Finally, to conclude discussing this alternative way to approach the refugee camp it is important to consider the research of Manuel Herz and the ETH Studio Basel about the Refugee Camps of Western

Sahara. The example of the South Saharan camps (Herz, 2012), born spontaneously as a refuge space, self-determined and self-managed, is an example of the potential alienation of the included space of the camp from the context in which it is inserted. The political situations that have led the Sahrawi population to live in a system of refugee camps in the Tinduf oasis are well expressed in Herz's research.

> The organisation of the Tindouf camps differs substantially from most refugee camps, in particular in the level of organisational autonomy. With limited outside interference, the refugees manage the activities and planning of camp life.
>
> The camps are divided into five wilaya (provinces), which derive their name from five cities of Western Sahara, now occupied territory: El Aaiun, Auserd, Smara, Dakhla and more recently also, Cape Bojador which has incorporated the small *February 27* camp, made up of women's boarding school; finally Rabouni which is the seat of the administrative offices.
>
> The settlements are spread over relatively large areas. El Aaiun, Smara, Auserd, Bojador and Rabouni are within an hour's drive from the city of Tindouf, while the Dakhla camp is 170 km from Tindouf in a southeast direction, almost on the border with Mali.
>
> (Herz, 2012, pp. 88, 109)

Around 170,000 people currently live in the Sahrawi refugee camps complex[16]. The camp has become a political manifesto for voluntary exile for the Sahrawis. Instead of being a non-place, it has acquired the value of a "home", even if temporary officially. The architectural language of the refugee camp, which arises from precariousness and the informal, mixed with that of the traditional Saharawi tents, is defined for different functions. The result is an urban context comprising systems and infrastructures, among which, in addition to the community ones (training and health), or those linked to work, Hertz identifies those linked to pastime and entertainment.

The refugee camp, understood as a homeland, a place of belonging, is possible beyond the infrastructures and the physical conformation.

> If we at the camps through the lenses of its inhabitants, we can certainly perceive the existence of urban qualities. Moreover, we can observe how the camp becomes a space where political aspiration are not only allowed to take place, but how the physical fabric

> of the camp becomes the very medium with which these political aspirations are expressed. In that sense the camp can be seen as expressing an essence of urbanity.
>
> (Herz, 2012, p. 18)

If the sense of urbanity can be that strong, then the study of the urban habitat becomes essential.

Possible Development

As we have seen so far, the nature of the refugee camp is complicated. The needs of an emergency collide with unpredictable timing, resulting in the context of indeterminate temporariness. The debate on this context is much more in-depth than expressed here. In particular, the question of quality of life, linked to the limitations of civil rights as a result of refugee status, is well illustrated in the works of other authors.

As much as one can aspire to normalisation, life inside the refugee camp results in a feeling of emergency and precariousness that generates discomfort (Agier, 2011). Furthermore, the larger the refugee camps are, the more the possibility of control by the bodies involved is lost, generating dangerous situations. Numerous reports highlight the low quality of living conditions in refugee camps: problems of health and salubrity of the spaces, violence and coercion on the weakest groups, and of denied rights.

An interesting report by *Chinedu Temple Obi* tells a clear account concerning escaping from the refugee camp's conditions. As Chinedu Temple Obi reports, about 60% of the refugees choose to live outside the camps, despite missing the advantages that belonging to the refugee camp brings (safety, food, shelter). The internal conditions are not worth baring with the disadvantages: excessive control, limited freedoms, unhealthy situations and isolation. Chinedu used difference-in-difference and propensity score matching methods over 2,399 Syrian refugee households, 50% of whom lived outside camps. This study measured the multidimensional quality of living (QOL) using two broad dimensions:

- "Life satisfaction" captures people's subjective well-being. It is often used when studying refugees because it requires respondents to reflect on and assess their life's happiness, including wealth, security, and hopes for the future.

- "Material living condition" captures households' objective living conditions and opportunities, including material deprivations that can be determined by counting the number of household assets such as beds, air conditioners, and cooking utensils, and the number of households living below the national poverty line. In addition, housing conditions can be captured by calculating overcrowding and satisfaction with accommodation services, such as water and electricity[17].

The results of the study show that living in a refugee camp reduces QOL for refugees:

- On average, refugees in camps are 36% more likely to live below the national extreme poverty line, meaning they find it difficult to meet daily basic needs.
- They are 37% more likely to live in overcrowded shelters.
- They own fewer household assets than refugees outside camps and are less satisfied with water, electricity, and sewerage access[18].

A further disaggregated result shows that living out-of-camp decreases female-headed household poverty more than male-headed households.

As Chinedu Temple Obi declares, this study sheds new light on the importance of understanding differences "in quality of life for refugees based on where they are living"[19]. However, the complexity of the social issue linked to refugee camps cannot be treated briefly, nor does will it be the subject of this discussion. We wanted to focus attention on the reality of the refugee camps because, from a morphological point of view, they align perfectly with what has already been expressed concerning temporary settlements. If we were to speak of the landscape of refugee camps, meaning it is a perceived and built image, we would have to translate it through the reading of the system of housing units, which inescapably dominates the context. The originating foundations illustrated above are clear from this point of view. It is the family unit that makes the refugee camp in mathematical aggregations. The grid responds to this need. Faced with this need, finding an alternative answer that is not naïve or random is difficult. For this reason, most projects to qualify the refugee camps from an architectural (as well as services) point of view concern the construction/reconstruction of collective services such as schools and hospitals.

In this last chapter, we suggest rethinking the aggregation system of housing units, starting from the parallels found between the various types of temporary cities. On the one hand, the relationship with the natural landscape is accidental. In fact, despite the indications of UNHCR regarding the need to consider the site's topography and conditions, the refugee camp's introverted nature does not react to the outside. There is no visual relationship or accessibility if not, as already said, accidental. Like *Burning Man* and *Kumbh Mela*, the "refugee camp" grows on a grid that looks at "itself" in perception and use.

The services within the camp are not designed to generate public space, and the concept of the public is insistent. It is no coincidence that one of the most emblematic examples of this within Hertz's work on the South Saharan Camps is that of the recognisability of some places of entertainment. These are manifestations of the appropriation of space by the community. These are obvious activities that fall outside the emergency manual.

It is interesting to note, as Michel Agier says, "if the idea of refuge could only be separated from the camp, then refuges could be considered as towns in the making" (Agier, 2011 p. 59). Therefore, it is nonetheless sensible to confront the refugee camp as if it were a city "tout court", while it must be valued in its exceptionality. In this exceptionality, determined primarily by its temporariness, we find the affinity with the accommodation facilities of open-air tourism. Even in these structures, public space is absent. Instead, the ordinary planning of the accommodation areas mathematically takes place (obviously with different numbers than those of the refugee camps). The space is divided into pitches and accessible areas for the housing units. Each unit corresponds to a pitch (the size of which varies from 90 to 150m^2)[20].

It is fair to consider that the morphology of the settlements affects human relationships, just as building the refugee camp, remaining completely extraneous to the future "citizens", contributes to increasing the distance between the inhabitants and the built-up area. The human dimension, mathematised by the UNHCR, is a minor subject with regard to variations in the refugee camps from the point of view of the settlement. The habitable space is developed with shelters made up of a single space. Depending on the situation, these same shelters evolve autonomously, changing the construction systems and generating a self-managed implementation.

As happens in the informal contexts of the slums, living is expressed through additions or mergers, always starting from the domestic nucleus of the "family". If, as we have seen, this mathematical departure is necessary, it is possible, in the face of a revision of the settlement premises of the camp, to reflect on alternative solutions. One of the criticisms of the refugee camp is that of applying a reference that is culturally distant from the places in which it is established. The architect Philipp Misselwitz noted that refugee camps were another form of a Roman encampment. Both models (refugee camp and encampment) are translated through a "functional diagram, orthogonal spatial organisations, temporary structures, surveillance and control devices such as watchtowers or perimeter fences" (Misselwitz, 2009, p. 57).

For example, an alternative reference to the Roman camp can be found in prehistoric African villages. These embryonic settlement systems perfectly represented an instinctive approach to living systems based on single-family dwellings. Constructing a protected context using the architectural units is an emblematic sign of these conditions. The domestic dimension, the individual or the essential family nucleus, becomes a unit with an edge to define the community space. Even today, it is possible to read in the plants of some African villages the inevitability of this approach. The distance between the outer world, the one of wild nature, is determined by the appearance of the human habitat. Even if positioned in the middle of the natural landscape, the villages define an "other" context by creating a virtual threshold, a limit consisting of a set of points. The example of the villages of the *Musgum*[21], who created their houses with compressed mud dried in the sun, defines the scope of "man" through the construction of the urban landscape made of homes and high walls. Each tribe created real clusters separated from the external natural context by employing a solid sign on the ground, a physical border, a wall and well-defined architecture.

Similarly, the Dogon[22] villages are undoubtedly among the most famous examples of this. The arrangement of housing structures follows an anthropomorphic principle oriented according to astronomical study. The reference to the human body is symbolic, but also emblematic of the settlement's identity towards the world/context in which it is inserted. The Dogon, rather than respecting a symmetrical design, present a natural space appropriation that adapts to the irregularities of the ground and imposes the human presence. The domestic architecture of the Dogon composes a very evident urban landscape. The living spaces are introverted and are developed with a fence, built with low walls and accompanied by small technical architecture (granaries), which define the image of a cluster inside the village.

> Generalising the traditional African architecture, the "rondavel" is a model of rural architecture widespread in the whole of Africa: several huts – each is a room – are built for a particular function around a central courtyard.
>
> (Tognon and Trabattoni, 2021, p. 66)

In its embryonic form, the village remains an interesting model of reading the relationship between a protected inside context and the external and dangerous one, at the scale of the small group. If abstracted from it's context and read from a dimensional and density perspective, the housing strategy of the villages is close to those of the clusters of open-air accommodation facilities. The theme of the cluster, understood as already explained, as a system of a few units that define a recognisable context, can easily be combined with that of the village. Just as in tourist villages, a dimension is sought that finds a balance between privacy and community; the settlement system of the cluster can determine a new form for the refugee camp.

Strategies

Three settlement strategies have previously been introduced: Topographic System, Introverted and Directed. These strategies define a triune relationship between the housing units, the prevailing landscape and the sphere of human relationships.

The pre-existing natural element becomes predominant in the topographical system, characterising the settlement system (level differences, orography, climate, winds). In the Introverted system, defining a privileged context determines a partial closure from the outside with the organisation of small enclaves. In the directed system, constructing an internal reference landscape organises a system of clusters homogeneously directed towards this new centrality.

By reconfiguring the terminology of the refugee camp, it is possible to highlight the similarities between them all better. According to the UNHCR guide, the area in which to establish the refugee camp must consider multiple factors, as we have seen, among which we find: the topography, the climate and the presence of communication routes. These three elements define the "main landscape" of the refugee camp or the pre-existence that determines its location. Obviously, the socio-political factors are equally fundamental, but the physical ones are the ones that define the image of the site. The restrictive nature of the refugee camp must also be considered, which determines an insurmountable limit beyond which the cessation of the refugee's rights persists.

In this way, climate and infrastructural systems represent the "landscape" systems that interfere within the refugee camp, which somehow break or modify the settlement grid. It is plausible to take these two elements as coordinates that give rise to a different settlement system linked to an organisational idea of the housing units that starts from the idea of the cluster as a transposition of the village dimension. Via this interpretation, the strategies for open-air accommodation facilities can give different settlement ideas, even while maintaining the pragmatic nature of the intervention:

- *Topographic/Climatic System:* Reading the natural landscape through its foundational characteristics is a traditional design approach. However, the climate can also be key to design if the morphology is binding. The sun's orientation, the direction of the winds and rainfall are strong factors on which to base the housing units' positioning and nature. First, managing radiation according to optimising the solar contribution defines the alignment of a settlement. Taking up an example from the African vernacular tradition linked to hot climates, the side most exposed to the sun is usually made with a closed wall in order to favour shade and ventilation. This closure often coincides with an opening on the opposite side toward a home enclosure. In a situation like the refugee camp, where the sizing does not envisage an external domestic space, generating compartments of housing units on the same or similar orientation is conceivable. This approach also suggests a rethinking of the technology of housing units. The principle of self-construction with low-technology or low-tech techniques (Trabattoni et al., 2021) would allow the "participatory" construction of efficient living spaces according to the climatic conditions. Michael Reynolds' Earthships is a striking example of an approach to sustainability through passive energy containment systems that can be built in self-construction and, therefore, autonomously.

Moreover, the example cited by Hertz concerning the Sharawi camps demonstrates how, if made possible, there is a desire to improve the construction of housing units within the refugee camp. Finally, systems such as raw earth, which can be used in almost any context, are excellent examples of how to apply architecture to the climate.

- *Introverted/Enclosure System:* Reorganising the housing units to manage intermediate collective spatialities between the family's private and the camp's public spaces. The determining scale factor in this strategy would allow the definition of shared and protected courtyards. The definition of a limit, or a margin, through the composition of the housing units would allow us to resume the spatiality mentioned above of the villages. The porous organisation of a system of units should allow the reorganisation of the private appurtenant space to generate a shared "collective" space. The problem of the number should be reviewed. Within the mathematical organisation of UNHCR, an intermediate dimension should be found between that of the family (4–6 people) and that of the communities (80 Families). A smaller cluster would allow better management of open spaces, giving rise to a relational need not necessarily linked to entertainment. Indeed, if, as in Hertz's example, the presence of spaces dedicated to activities other than occupational ones is symptomatic of the presence of a stable community, providing an incidental spatiality linked to the family could be a qualifying solution. With that form of neighbourhood security, the controlled open space refers to Jane Jacobs's idea of the street as a collective place.
- *Directed System/Square*: Taking the infrastructural system as a focal point, understood not only as a communication system, but also as a connection and aggregation system, the housing units could generate a sequence of spaces, which can be modulated to the dimensions of choice. This way, the refugee camp could be organised to enhance the void, understood as a potential organisational space. The number of units should exceed that of the introverted cluster to define an aggregative place that unites several families and sectors. As shown by Hertz's work on the South Saharan Camps, the value of the aggregation space is determined by undefined functions. Recreational or commercial activities can find a place in these spaces. In order to define collective meeting places alternative to infrastructural ones, a spatial system could

TOPOGRAPHIC/ CLIMATIC SYSTEM

THE UNITS CAN BE SETTLED DOWN BY TAKING AS REFERENCE SOME CHARACTERISTICS OF THE CONTEXT, SUCH AS:
.TOPOGRAPHY
.WHEATHER
.SUN ORIENTATION
.WIND

MAINTAINING THE ORIGINAL UNIT BY UNHCR IS POSSIBLE TO ORGANIZE THE NEW SETTLEMENT ORIENTATION KEEPING TWO DIRECTIONS, BOTH VALUABLE, THAT CAN GENERATE THE VILLAGE IDEA.

Figure 3.4 Topographic Diagram

INTROVERTED/ ENCLOSURE SYSTEM

THE UNITS CAN BE ORGANIZED IN SMALL CLUSTER THAT CAN BE REPETED

EACH CLUSTER BEACEM THE SPACE OF A COMMUNITY AND BY THIS WAY IS POSSIBLE TO GENERATE A COMPLEX SISTEM OF LANDSCAPE.
THE DIVISION BETWEEN INTERIOR AND EXTERIOR BECAME MORE CLEAR.
THE SMALLER SPACES HAVE MORE CONTROL E SO THEY CAN BE PERCEIVED AS SAFER, SHARING A LITTLE PART OF ITS PRIVACY

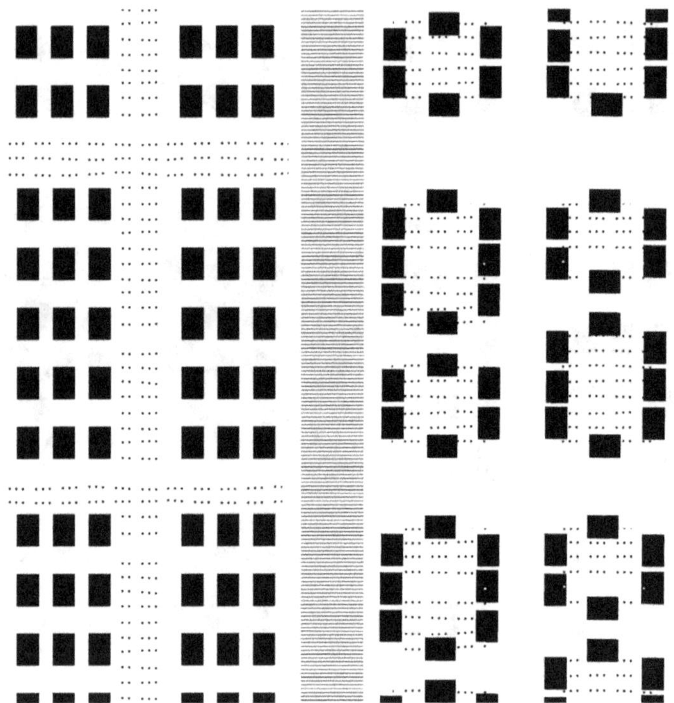

Figure 3.5 Introverted Diagram

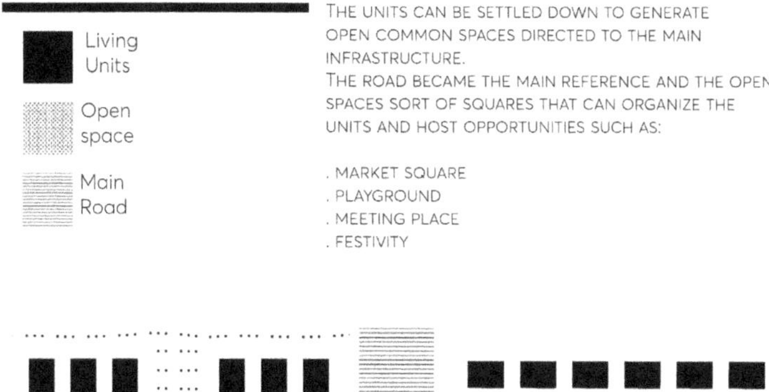

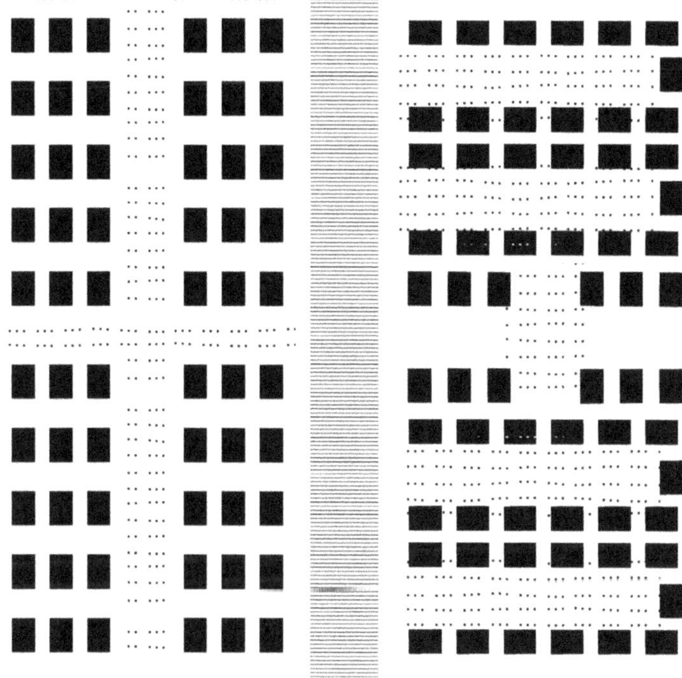

Figure 3.6 Directed Diagram

be generated that qualifies the extra-domestic space. Currently, this "collective" function is delegated to services; schools and hospitals, when they are built in these sectors, are often understood as symbolic community places. The safety of these spaces makes them ideal as social containers. However, as informal contexts teach, large empty spaces can be an opportunity for improvised or commercial activities. Places of this nature, linked to the infrastructure to ensure immediate accessibility, could become a new internal landscape of reference on which to build the identity of the refugee camp, regardless of the length of its life.

Notes

1 "La difficile ricerca di una normalità: la vita in un campo profughi" (The difficult search for normality: life in a refugee camp), https://www.ispionline.it/it/tag/campi-profughi Accessed online 28 March 2023.

2 United Nations High Commissioner for Refugees is the United Nations agency specialised in the management of refugees; it provides them with international protection and material assistance, and pursues durable solutions to their plight. It is the world's leading frontline organisation for saving lives and protecting the rights of millions of refugees. It was founded on 14 December 1950 by the General Assembly in Geneva, and started operations on 1 January 1951. It assists over 60 million people and has won two Nobel Peace Prizes, in 1954 and 1981 respectively. https://www.unhcr.org/history-of-unhcr.html.

3 UNRWA (United Nations Relief and Works Agency for Palestine Refugees in the Near East), was established in 1948 following the Arab–Israeli war. It is a relief, development, education, health care, social services and emergency relief agency to over five million Palestinian refugees living in Jordan, Lebanon, Syria, the West Bank and the Gaza Strip. It is the only agency dedicated only to helping refugees from a specific region or conflict. It is separate from UNHCR, the UN refugee agency, which is the only other UN agency dedicated to helping refugees and cares for all other refugees around the world (Herz, 2012).

4 Numerous essays and articles have been written on the Palestinian question, among others see the text by Ilan Pappè and Naom Chomsky, *Ultima Fermata Gaza, Where Israel's war with the Palestinians takes us 2015.*

5 UNHCR Emergency Handbook, p. 1.

6 https://www.unrefugees.org/news/refugee-camps-explained/#What%20is%20a%20refugee%20camp?

7 "Sites for planned camps should be selected in consultation with various sectors, including WASH, protection and supply, and with technical

specialists such as hydrologists, surveyors, planners, engineers, and environmental engineers", https://www.unrefugees.org/news/refugee-camps-explained/#What%20is%20a%20refugee%20camp?

8 The Sphere Project, now known as Sphere, was created in 1997 by a group of humanitarian non-governmental organisations and the Red Cross and Red Crescent Movement. Its aim was to improve the quality of their humanitarian responses and to be accountable for their actions (see *The Sphere Handbook*).

9 From the Glossary of the UNHCR Global Report 2005.

10 The proportion of the world's population who have been displaced continues to rise. One per cent of the world's population – or 1 in 97 people – is now forcibly displaced. This compares with 1:159 in 2010 and 1:174 in 2005 as the increase in the world's forcibly displaced population continued to outpace global population growth... . Climate change and natural disasters can exacerbate threats that force people to flee within their country or across international borders. The interplay between climate, conflict, hunger, poverty and persecution creates increasingly complex emergencies (UNHCR Global Trends, 2019).

11 UNHCR Dadaab Refugee Complex, https://www.unhcr.org/ke/dadaab-refugee-complex (Accessed online 1 June 2023).

12 https://www.unhcr.org/news/stories/jordans-zaatari-refugee-camp-10-facts-10-years (Accessed online 1 June 2023).

13 The record disputed with Dadaab is overcome because the latter reaches more than 200,000 refugees but only by merging three camps. Kakuna reaches around 190,000 refugees in one camp alone.

14 https://www.unhcr.org/ke/kakuma-refugee-camp.

15 https://wearealight.org/6-cool-things-in-one-of-the-oldest-refugee-camps/.

16 UNHCR, "Sahrawi Refugees in Tindouf, Algeria: Total In-Camp Population – 2018".

17 "How refugees' decision to live in or outside a camp affects their quality of life", https://blogs.worldbank.org/dev4peace/how-refugees-decision-live-or-outside-camp-affects-their-quality-life. This work is part of the program "Building the Evidence on Forced Displacement: A Multi-Stakeholder Partnership". The program is funded by UK aid from the United Kingdom's Foreign, Commonwealth, and Development Office (FCDO). It is managed by the World Bank Group (WBG) and was established in partnership with the United Nations High Commissioner for Refugees (UNHCR).

18 Ibid.

19 Ibid.

20 This data derives from a market survey linked to the professional activity of the Camp Design Studio, which designs campsites and accommodation facilities. There is no specific law that determines this sizing.

21 An ethnic group in the far north province of Cameroon.

22 An African population living in Mali.

Conclusions

That which is illustrated in the discussion of this book highlights the role of open-air accommodation facilities within the study of open-air settlement systems. As we have seen, the construction of a temporary settlement entails the creation of a relationship between the landscape, its complexity, the housing system and time. When time is very short, the relationship with the landscape is indirect. The reference landscape system is managed as an immutable monad, actively used but not modified. The landscape acts as a backdrop and, as such, determines the context of the temporary settlement, but does not significantly insist on its morphology.

The examples shown propose highly geometric urban morphologies linked to pragmatic choices of intensive land occupation while working with removable buildings. We can deduce the programmatic choice of concentrating the built-up area in order to leave the landscape free, which is the real place to live. This happens in Black Rock City during the *Burning Man Festival*, which concentrates on relationships and artistic expression in the void of the desert, as it does in the versions of the *Kumbh Mela* that use the river as the centre of the main religious activities.

However, when this same approach is applied over a much more extended period, it generates contexts of low housing quality due to multiple factors, as in the emblematic case of refugee camps. These temporary places approach the existing landscape in a detached way, as in the cases described in the first chapter, even in the face of the political constraints underlying the foundation of the camp. Similarly, they manage the urban morphology intensively, pragmatically optimising the living space. However, by changing the time factor from short

DOI: 10.4324/9781003468530-5

to long and removing the relationship with the landscape outside the settlement, which is no longer usable, in the face of the limits imposed by the camp management, the human habitat loses quality, generating that which is described in Chapter 3. With this, we do not mean to say that the urban form is the cause of the inconvenience of a complex situation, such as that of the UNHCR camps, but only to underline how, from the point of view of the construction of the settlement, the lack of enhancement of the relationship with the landscape as a function of time contributes to aggravate that same situation.

Open-air accommodation facilities are an example of a temporary city in which the relationship with the landscape with regard to the "time of use" can give satisfactory results. The relationship between the "time of use" and the landscape is complex and must therefore be resolved in a non-superficial way. The traditional approach, linked to the perception of the prevailing natural element, loses its value when the perception of the landscape fails. The proposed design strategies start from the assumption of the need to build a landscape inside the facilities structures that enhances the settlement, starting with the presence of the Maxi-Caravans. The problems related to over-tourism and the conservation of the natural landscape must be conveyed within these strategies. However, again, we are not proposing definitive solutions for environmental compatibility, but effective methods for building contexts suited to requirements.

The dual relationship with the landscape (mainly and internally) and with time (seasonal and industrial products) determines the coding of a renewable settlement system based on collecting small aggregative units. The increasingly incisive presence of removable housing units imposes a disciplinary approach that reflects on the construction of the landscape. The enhancement of empty spaces, or interstitial spaces, as a function of the construction of the landscape, leads to the definition of repeatable strategies.

Working with the topography, the aggregation and the landscape reconstruction are effective systems to compensate for the scale factor. However, it is clear that in tiny hospitality establishments, the value of this approach becomes liminal. In more extensive accommodation facilities, on the other hand, the need to build a landscape that determines the reference context of one or more clusters of housing units is an opportunity to reflect on living in the natural environment. In these places, therefore, the valorisation of the existing landscape passes through the coding of a new landscape, which changes over time. This dynamic approach is proposed here in an embryonic way, working on the relationship between the elements without going into the merits of the actual construction of the landscape.

The theme of sustainability, both contingent and necessary, cannot only be solved through a reworking of the settlement system, but must be faced on multiple levels: energy, material, management of resources and waste. These issues, now acquired by the open-air tourism market, are tackled in an isolated and timely manner, with some interesting exceptions, such as in the case of the sustainability charter promoted by the municipality of Cavallino Treporti[1]. This administration, which represents one of Italy's most important tourist destinations with several presences and Maxi-Caravans installed, has recently drawn up a voluntary environmental compensation plan specific to open-air accommodation facilities.

The settlement approach proposed in this discussion, while not being decisive, wants to supportive of these accommodation facilities. In its historical and market evolution, the campsite has ceased to be a simple exercise of temporary land occupation for tourism purposes. It has become a habitable dwelling in all respects.

The inherent opportunity in these places is linked to the cognitive act that can accompany the housing one, linked to the rediscovery of nature consciously, and linked to the enhancement of the landscape and its protection.

Note

1 Dichiarazione ambientale. Aggiornata al 30/06/2021. Documento redatto dal Comune di Cavallino Treporti (VE) e secondo i requisiti EMAS, Reg. (UE) 2009/1221, Reg. (UE) 2017/1505, Reg. (UE) 2018/2026, Codice NACE 2: 84.11, Rev. 07 del 03.12.2021 - Environmental statement. Updated 06/30/2021. Document drawn up by the Municipality of Cavallino Treporti (VE) and in accordance with the EMAS requirements. Reg. (EU) 2009/1221. Reg. (EU) 2017/1505. Reg. (EU) 2018/2026. NACE Code 2: 84.11. Rev 07 of 03.12.2021.

Bibliography

Monographs

Agier, M., *Managing the Undesirables: Refugee Camps and Humanitarian Government*, Malden, USA, Polity, 1st edition, 2011.

Barabara, A., *Sensi, tempo e architettura*, Milano, Postmedia books, 2012.

Bauman, Z., *La società dell'incertezza*, Bologna, il Mulino, 1999.

Bauman, Z., *Liquid Modernity*, 2000, Roma-Bari, *Modernità liquida*, Laterza, 2002.

Berizzi, C. and Trabattoni, L., *Mobile Home per il turismo all'aria aperta. Storia evolutiva*, Tortona, Vicolo del pavone, 2019.

Bey, H., *T.A.Z. La Zona Autonoma Temporanea*, Milano, Shake Edizioni, 1993, new edition Shake Edizioni, 2020.

Braggs, S. and Harris, D., *Sun, Sea and Sand: The Great British Seaside Holiday*, Stroud, Tempus, 2006.

Burckhardt, L. *Il falso è l'autentico Politica, paesaggio, design, architettura, pianificazione, pedagogia*, Italy, Quodlibet, 2019.

Burton, R., *The Anatomy of Melancholy*, 1621, *Anatomia della malinconia, a cura di Stefania D'Agata D'Ottavi*, Torino, Collezione I Millenni, 2023.

Cangelli, E., *Ecocamp, il campeggio ecologico e la riqualificazione ambientale della costa*, Firenze, Alinea, 2006.

Cappai, A., *Dal al neorealismo italiano al landscape planning americano: La fondazione del paesaggio turistico della Costa Smeralda* – tesi di dottorato Universitat Politecnica de Catalunya Departament d'Urbanisme i Ordenació del Territori Febbraio, 2014, p. 52.

Clément, G., *Manifesto del Terzo paesaggio*, Macerata, Quodlibet, 2004.

Clément, G., *Il giardiniere planetario*, Milano, 22 Publishing, 2008.

Clément, G., *Il giardino in movimento*, Macerata, Quodlibet, 2011.

Comi, C.U., *Spazio, tempo e città*, Milano, Maggioli editore, 2009, p. 21.

Corbin, A., *L'invenzione del mare. L'occidente e il fascino della spiaggia (1750–1840)*, Marsilio, Venezia, 1990.

Dagnino, A., *I Nuovi Nomadi. Pionieri della mutazione, culture evolutive, nuove professioni*, Roma, Castelvecchi, 1996.

Desportes, M., *Paesaggi in movimento. Trasporti e percezione dello spazio tra XVIII e XX secolo*, Milano, Libri Scheiwiller, illustrated edition, 2008.

Dobraszczyk, P., *Architecture and Anarchism: Building without Authority*, London, Paul Holberton Publishing Ltd, 2021.

Fonti, A. and Mameli, M., *Luigi Snozzi, un'autobiografia architettonica*, Milano, Franco Angeli, 2012, p. 42, 43.

Ginanni, F., *Istoria civile e naturale delle pinete ravennati*, Roma, Giovanni Generoso Salomoni, 1774.

Gupta, O., *Encyclopaedia of India, Pakistan and Bangladesh*, New Delhi, Gyan Publishing House, 2006, p. 1330.

Herz, M., *From Camp to City, Refugee Camps of the Western Sahara*, Baden, Lars Müller Publishers, 2012.

i Casanovas, R.B. *Rosa Barba 1970–2000: works and words*, ASFLOR Ediciones, Sitges, DL, 2010.

Ingle, R., *Thomas Cook of Leicester*, Burford, Headstart History, 1991.

Inskeep, E., *Tourism planning, an integrated and sustainable development approach*, Hoboken, John Wiley & Sons Inc, 1991, p. 308.

Koolhaas, R. and Olbrich, H., *Project Japan: Metabolism Talks...*, Colonia, Taschen America Llc, 2011.

Marcenaro, R., *Mobile City*, Milan, Franco Angeli, 2011.

McQuaid, M., *Envisioning Architecture: Drawings from The Museum of Modern Art*, New York, The Museum of Modern Art, 2002, p. 150.

Mehrotra, R. and Vera, F., *Kumbh Mela: Mapping the Ephemeral MEGACITY*, New Delhi, Niyogi Books, 2015.

Mitchell, W.J.T., *Landscape and Power*, Chicago, University of Chicago Press, second edition, 2002.

Neufert E. and Neufert, P., *Neufert Architects' Data*, Fourth Edition, Hoboken, Wiley-Blackwell, 2012.

Olmert, M., *Milton's Teeth and Ovid's Umbrella: Curiouser & Curiouser Adventures in History*, New York, Simon & Schuster, 1996, p. 170.

Oudolf, P. and Kingsbury, N., *Planting: A New Perspective*, Portland, Timber press, 2013.

Rahola, F., *Zone definitivamente temporanee. I luogi dell'umanità in eccesso*, Italy, Ombre Corte, 2003.

Rudofsky, B., *Architecture without Architects: a Short Introduction to Non-pedigreed Architecture*, New York, Doubleday, 1964.

Sennett, R., *Costruire e abitare. Etica per la città*, Milano, Giangiacomo Feltrinelli Editore, 2018.

Sezgin, E. and Yolal, M., *Golden Age of Mass Tourism: Its History and Development*, Eskişehir, Anadolu University, 2012, p. 73–77.

Thoreau, H.D., *Walden ovvero Vita nei boschi 1854*, (con testo inglese a fronte), a cura di Franco Venturi, Milano, La Vita Felice, 2016.

Tognon, A. and Trabattoni, L., *Necessary Architecture: Raw Earth Solutions for a Common House in Niger*, Oxford, CRC Press; 1st edition, 2021.

Tost, X. and Duran, A., *Arquitecturas del turismo informal. El habitar ludcio en la naturaleza*, Ediciones Asimétricas, 2020.

Trabattoni, L., Capotorto, M. and Berizzi, C., *Progettare lo spazio minimo delle maxi-caravan. Qualità, ergonomia e fruizione degli ambienti interni* , AUDe; Crippacampeggio srl, 2024, ISBN: 979221058345.

Trillo, C., *Territori del turismo. Tra utopia e atopia*, Firenze, Alinea, 2003.

Urry J., *The Tourist Gaze*, Los Angeles; London, Sage Publications Ltd, 2002.

Ward, C. and Hardy, D., *Goodnight Campers! The History of the British Holiday Camp*, London, Routledge, 1998.

Articles

Berizzi C., Capotorto, M., Terlicher, G. and Trabattoni, L., "Coastal Vulnerability: Sustainable Settlements for Outdoor Tourism", in *Design for Vulnerable Communities*, Berlin, Springer, 2022, pp. 283–304, DOI: 10.1007/978-3-030-96866-3_15.

Berizzi, C., Capotorto, M., Terlicher, G. and Trabattoni, L., "The Sustainability of the Campsite as It Relates to Morphology, Climate and Landscape", *Highlights of Sustainability*, 2(4), 185–206, September 2023, DOI: 10.54175/hsustain2040014.

Berizzi C., Capotorto, M., Mazurkiewicz, M., Terlicher, G. and Trabattoni, L., "Summer City: Campsites as a New Ecological Approach to Sustainable Living", in *Environmental Challenges in Civil Engineering II*, Cham, Springer, 2023, pp. 211–225, DOI:10.1007/978-3-031-26879-3_17.

Berizzi, C., Nirta, S., Terlicher, G. and Trabattoni, L., "Sustainable and Affordable Prefabricated Construction: Developing a Natural, Recycled, and Recyclable Mobile Homem", *Sustainability*, 13(15), July 2021, DOI: 10.3390/su13158296.

Blei, D., "Come sono nate le vacanze al mare", *ilpost*, 17 July 2016, Available at https://www.ilpost.it/2016/07/17/come-sono-nate-le-vacanze-al-mare/.

Capotorto, M. and Trabattoni, L., "The city of entertainment as an experimentation field for improving the daily public space", XXIX Conference Of The International Seminar On Urban Form 2022 Łódź – Kraków | September 6–11, 2022 Urban Redevelopment and Revitalisation A Multidisciplinary Perspective, in *Book of Abstracts*.

Carlisle, L., "Jordan's Za'atari refugee camp: 10 facts at 10 years", *UNHCR*, 29 July 2022, Available at https://www.unhcr.org/news/stories/2022/7/62e2a95d4/jordans-zaatari-refugee-camp-10-facts-10-years.html, Accessed on 28 March 2023.

Deyong, S., "Walking City: Archigram and the Pursuit of Style", in *The Companions to the History of Architecture, Volume IV* (edited by David Leatherbarrow and Alexander Eisenschmidt), Hoboken, Wiley-Blackwell, 2017.

Fischer, A., "Working in the Desert, The Significance of Labour Performances among Tuareg Nomads in the Algerian Sahara" *Anthropos*, 112(2), 574–583, 2017, DOI: 10.5771/0257-9774-2017-2-574.

Geuze, A. and Skjonsberg, M., "Second Nature: New Territories for the Exiled", in *Infrastructure and Landscape: Case Studies by SWA*, Basel, Berlin and Boston, Birkenhauser, 2013.

Grassi, S., "Rivista Quadrimestrale Di Diritto Dell'ambiente", *Quarterly Journal of Environmental Law*, 2017(3).

Hailey, C., "Camps: A Guide to 21st-Century Space; Campsite: Architectures of Duration and Place; and A Manufactured Wilderness: Summer Camps and the Shaping of American Youth, 1890–1960", *Journal of Architectural Education*, 64(2), 176–178, February 2011, DOI: 10.1111/j.1531-314X.2010.01148.x.

Maisah, "Saudi Arabia Has Allocated Mina Camps For 1 million Pilgrims", *The Islamic Information*, 2 June 2022, Available at https://theislamicinformation.com/news/saudi-arabia-allocated-mina-camps-hajj-2022.

Manca, E., "Persuasione, Tourist Gaze E Turismo Di Lusso, Modi comunicativi e culture a confronto", Lingue Linguaggi, 20, 215–237, January 2017, DOI: 10.1285/i22390359v20p215.

Merleau-Ponty, M., *Cézanne's Doubt*, Evanston, Northwestern University Press, 1945 [1964], Available at https://faculty.uml.edu/rinnis/cezannedoubt.pdf.

Misselwitz P. and Hanafi, S., "TESTING A NEW PARADIGM: UNRWA'S CAMP IMPROVEMENT PROGRAMME". *Refugee Survey Quarterly*, 28(2/3), 360–388, 2009.

Mucelli, E., "Houses In The Wood To Enjoy The Sun And The Starsagathón", *International Journal of Architecture, Art and Design*, 2(2017), DOI: 10.19229/2464-9309/2212017.

Rogers, E.N., "Homo Additus Naturae", *Casabella continuità*, 283, January 1964.

Saha, K. and Khare, R., "A Geospatial Approach to Conserving Cultural Heritage Tourism at Kumbh Mela Events in India", in *Tourism, Cultural Heritage and Urban Regeneration*, Cham, Springer, 2020, DOI: 10.1007/978-3-030-41905-9_9.

Swanson, A., "The weird origins of going to the beach", *The Washington Post*, 3 July 2016 [online], Available at https://www.washingtonpost.com/news/wonk/wp/2016/07/03/the-weird-origins-of-going-to-the-beach/, Accessed on 29 July 2022.

Tost, X.M., "Architecture for Informal Tourism – Mild Occupation of Landscape through Campsites", Athens, ATINER's Conference Paper Series, No: ARC2015-1589, 2015.

Trabattoni, L., Berizzi, C., Battistella, A., and Luisi, S. (2021). Le tecnologie appropriate nell'architettura d'emergenza. *TERRITORIO*, 93, 139–146. https://doi.org/10.3280/TR2020-093021

Young, T., "Why Americans Invented The RV: In 1915, New Creature Comforts Created by Technology Merged with the Back to Nature Movement", *Smithsonian*, 2018b, Available at https://www.smithsonianmag.com/innovation/brief-history-rv-180970195/.

Wallace, G. and Russell, A., "Eco-cultural tourism as a means for the sustainable development of culturally marginal and environmentally sensitive regions", *Tourist Studies*, 4(3), 235–254, https://doi.org/10.1177/1468797604057326.

Wilkinson, F., "La vita nei campi base dell'Everest", *National Geographic*, 27 May 2020, Available at https://www.nationalgeographic.it/viaggi/2020/05/la-vita-nei-campi-base-delleverest.

Young, T., "The religious roots of America's love for camping, how a minister's accidental bestseller launched the country's first outdoor craze", *Zocalo Public Square*, 2018a, Available at https://www.zocalopublicsquare.org/.

Documents

"Agenda Landscha", p. 8.

Centro di studi sociali, documentazione, informazione e azione e Ufficio centrale di beneficenza e servizi sociali, "Informazione francese", Vita sociale: cahiers du CEDIAS, July 1966, pp. 333–334 (online) Available at https://gallica.bnf.fr/ark:/12148/bpt6k6315096n/f19, Accessed on 9 March 2022.

"Constitution of the Italian State" [Costituzione dello stato italiano.]

Convenzione Europea del Paesaggio, "Codice dei Beni Culturali e del Paesaggio, Explanatory Report", ETS 176 – European Landscape Convention.

"Costituzione di Weimar", 11 August 1919, Available at http://www.dircost.unito.it/cs/pdf/19190811_germaniaWeimar_ita.pdf.

"Décret n° 2007-18 du 5 janvier 2007 pris pour l'application de l'ordonnance n° 2005-1527 du 8 décembre 2005 relative au permis de construire et aux autorisations d'urbanisme) // Section IV, sous-section 2".

Dispositivo dell'art. 142, "Codice dei beni culturali e del paesaggio Codice dei beni culturali e del paesaggio, PARTE TERZA – Beni paesaggistici, Titolo I – Tutela e valorizzazione, Capo II – Individuazione dei beni paesaggistici".

"Global Code of Ethics for Tourism", adopted by resolution A/RES/406(XIII) at the thirteenth WTO General Assembly (Santiago, Chile, 27 September–1 October 1999).

"Il Codice Mondiale di Etica del Turismo Italiano" (allegato 1 del decreto legislativo 79/2011).

"Landscape Character Assessment: Guidance for England and Scotland (2002)", Scottish Natural Heritage and The Countryside Agency.

"l'Osservatorio Turismo Outdoor | Previsioni Estate 2022", report created by Human Company and Thrends.

Ujjain Smart City Proposal, 2016, Ministry of Urban Development, Government of India.

UNHCR, *Handbook for Emergencies*, Third Edition, 2007.

UNHCR, "KISEDP, KALOBEYEI INTEGRATED SOCIO-ECONOMIC DEVELOPMENT PLAN IN TURKANA WEST", 2018, https://www.unhcr.org/ke/wp-content/uploads/sites/2/2018/12/KISEDP.pdf

Various authors, "Documenti di vita italiana", vol. 24, Roma, Presidenza del Consiglio dei ministri, Servizio delle informazioni, p. 939. Accessed on 19 February 2020.

World Tourism Organization (UNWTO), Centre of Expertise Leisure, Tourism & Hospitality; NHTV Breda University of Applied Sciences; and NHL Stenden University of Applied Science, "'Overtourism'? Understanding and Managing Urban Tourism Growth beyond Perceptions: Executive Summary", UNWTO, Madrid, 2018, Available at https://www.e-unwto.org/doi/epdf/10.18111/9789284420070, p. 4, Accessed on 25 August 2020.

Websites

Harvey, Larry, *Burning Man's 10 Principles*, 2004, https://burningman.org/about/10-principles/

http://ruralstudio.org/2020-20k-home/

http://www.dircost.unito.it

http://www.isle-of-man.com/manxnotebook/tourism/ccamp/index.htm

https://ec.europa.eu/eurostat/en/web/products-eurostat-news/-/ddn-20210401-1

https://group.humancompany.com/it/news/human-company-stagione-2022-record

https://sfaiph304.files.wordpress.com

https://www.beniculturalionline.it/post.php?n=1522

https://www.britannica.com/place/Field-of-Cloth-of-Gold

https://www.clubmed.it/

https://www.digitouring.it/

https://www.ioamoiviaggi.it/vacanza-in-toscana-nella-pineta-di-roccamare/

https://www.treccani.it/vocabolario/turismo/

https://www.zocalopublicsquare.org/

Pirelli, rivista di informazione e di tecnica, Available at http://search.fondazionepirelli.org/bookreader/riviste/RivistaPirelli/1968_9.html?q=&start=79&lang=it&fbclid=IwAR21Job517xv501CswiFoLVBiq8Ax6Q5CZr9ifLRN7x-_UUbK_5uRL-wxxw, Accessed on 9 March 2022.

Venice Biennale 2016, “Ephemeral Urbanism: Cities in Constant Flux”, curated by Rahul Mehrotra and Felipe Vera. Video by Henry Bauer and Cristian Pino Anguita, Available at https://www.youtube.com/watch?v=N8uu3VW_A48

Index

For Product Safety Concerns and Information please contact our EU representative GPSR@taylorandfrancis.com
Taylor & Francis Verlag GmbH, Kaufingerstraße 24, 80331 München, Germany

www.ingramcontent.com/pod-product-compliance
Lightning Source LLC
LaVergne TN
LVHW010915110826
845149LV00013B/2368

* 9 7 8 1 0 3 2 7 4 2 8 5 4 *